completely revised second edition

serves ONE

by Toni Lydecker

Lake Isle Press

New York

Published by:

Lake Isle Press, Inc.

16 West 32nd Street, Suite 10-B

New York, NY 10001

(212) 273-0796

E-mail: lakeisle@earthlink.net

Distributed to the trade by:

National Book Network (NBN), Inc.

4501 Forbes Boulevard, Suite 200

Lanham, MD 20706

1 (800) 462-6420

www.nbnbooks.com

Library of Congress Control Number: 2005929073

ISBN: 1-891105-14-0

Food photography copyright © 2005 Dasha Wright

Book and cover design: Ellen Swandiak

This book is available at special sales discounts for bulk purchases as premiums or special editions, including personalized covers. For more information, contact the publisher at (212) 273-0796 or by e-mail, lakeisle@earthlink.net

Second Edition

Manufactured in the United States of America

10 9 8 7 6 5 4 3 2 1

acknowledgments

Without the warm encouragement of Hiroko Kiiffner, president of Lake Isle Press, I wouldn't have had the opportunity to write this new edition of *Serves One*. I'm also grateful to Dasha Wright for her appealing photographs of single-serving dishes, Ellen Swandiak for her imaginative design and Pimpila Thanaporn for her skillful management of the production process.

Many thanks to friends and family who shared recipes and practical advice about solo cooking. Kate Lydecker, my older daughter, helped develop and test a number of recipes, as well as helping me judge their appeal to her twenty-something peers. And my husband Kent and younger daughter Mary were always ready to taste and critique yet another round of serves-one recipes.

In memory of Joyce Hudson, my mother

table of contents

author's note

Eight years ago, I wrote the first edition of *Serves One* with the goal of helping anyone, from a beginner to a veteran cook, turn out an appetizing meal for one.

Since the first edition came out, the need for small-scale approaches to home cooking has only increased. The American household is shrinking, with more than 60 percent of the population living alone or with just one other person. Larger households are in the minority, and yet virtually all of the cookbooks on the market operate in a "serves four" mode. *Serves One* doesn't, of course. Instead, this new and completely revised edition is packed with advice on shopping, kitchen equipment, and staples for solo cooking.

Recognizing how busy people are, I wanted the recipes to be very approachable—to deliver great-tasting, wholesome meals that don't take a ton of time to make. Some favorites from the first edition have been simplified in pursuit of this goal, and many others are entirely new. The recipes also reflect the growing availability of products that make single-portion cooking easier or more interesting: high-quality prewashed lettuce and other produce, and the truly amazing array of seasonings, condiments, and ethnic ingredients (especially Asian) now on the market, to cite just two examples.

I hope *Serves One* will be well thumbed by college students and other young people living on their own for the first time, as well as mid-career singles, empty nesters, newly divorced or widowed people, and retirees learning how to downsize meals. In addition, I believe that this book will prove useful to couples and to people who eat alone only occasionally—in other words, just about everyone could benefit from serves-one strategies!

intro

I used to be puzzled by those who dismissed the idea of making a real meal for one person. "Way too much trouble" and "I'm just too busy" are among their responses, but I've come to believe that the most potent reason is a vague feeling that it's wrong to be eating alone. Our society celebrates the importance of connecting with friends and family over the dinner table—and rightly so—but the pleasures of solitary dining are rarely acknowledged.

Those pleasures are considerable, and they deserve to be more widely known. For one thing, whether you eat alone routinely or just once in a while, you have a great deal of company. More than two-thirds of Americans eat a meal by themselves a few days a week, or even more often. In other words, solo dining is more the norm than is the ideal of communal meals that we carry around in our heads. So why not relax and enjoy the experience?

For me, that enjoyment comes from sitting down to a meal worth savoring. I enjoy a restaurant meal or food from my favorite takeout place (which happens to be Indian) as much as the next person, but not every day. Frozen entrées and most other prepared foods can be monotonous and less than fabulous. So that means heading to the kitchen for a worthwhile cause: treating myself to a good meal. My intent with *Serves One* is to share some of the solo meals I love, along with shopping tips and other strategies that make it easier and more satisfying to cook for oneself.

I'm not talking about meals that take hours to make, and there's room for flexibility. One night you might sit down to a chicken and olive ragout that took half an hour to make. On a busier day, the homemade touch could be as simple as freshly toasted croutons sprinkled over the salad you picked up on the way home, or your own marinated olives on a plate of cheese, crackers, and fruit.

The recipes in *Serves One* are grouped informally, reflecting the way most of us like to eat when we're on our own. In deference to the fact that the cook is also the cleanup crew, many are all-in-one meals requiring minimal cleanup—main-course salads, simple stir-fries, and beans-and-rice combos, for example. Other chapters offer fresh takes on pizza and pasta, savory soups, chicken and shrimp dishes, inventive sandwiches, and a few irresistible treats.

Most recipes yield just one serving, but I couldn't see any point in being rigid about this. When making certain soups or stews, it's so easy to make a little extra, and so nice to have it on hand. In such cases, the recipe explains how to divide and store the extra servings for other meals.

Each recipe spells out the amount of preparation time and cooking time required so that you can make an informed decision about whether to make it on a particular day. A typical recipe takes about ten minutes prep time and ten minutes cooking time. If you haven't cooked much for yourself, I think you'll be pleasantly surprised at how much easier and faster it is than preparing meals for a group. There's less of everything—smaller quantities of ingredients, less chopping and, quite often, shorter cooking times.

Although standard measurements and instructions are given, seasonings such as salt, black pepper, and red pepper flakes are often "to taste." After all, you're using just a pinch or a dash, and the exact amount depends very much on your individual preferences and dietary requirements.

The spirit behind *Serves One* is not slavish measuring and rule following, but inspiration that leads to improvisation and adjustments as you discover a style of cooking that pleases you. There are many reasons to cook for yourself, and this book will help you seize the opportunity.

1 It's a chance to pamper yourself.

You'd treat yourself to a manicure or massage, right? So take time to indulge in a good, home-cooked meal.

2 Do it for your health.

You're going to be buying fresh produce and other wholesome ingredients to make these recipes, and that's better than a diet heavy on prepared foods.

3 Control what you eat.

In a restaurant, you don't see that extra glob of butter or the shower of salt the chef swirls into the sauce on your entrée. At home, you can decide what goes in your food—and how much goes on the plate.

4 Splurge a little, affordably.

When you don't have to share, you can afford the best steak, an exquisite cheese, and those beautiful microgreens.

cook for yourself

5 Bring more variety into your life.

You deserve a break from the umpteenth bowl of cereal or can of tuna eaten at your kitchen counter.

6 For once, your taste is all that counts.

If you love spicy foods, add an extra garlic clove or spoonful of salsa. And if you've always hated bell peppers, go right ahead and boycott them.

7 Eat in style.

At least once in a while, set the table with your best dishes, and eat a tranquil, candlelight dinner.

8 Cooking can be therapeutic.

Not to mention, fun! Tune your radio to your favorite station, pour a glass of "cooking wine," and unwind while creating a great meal.

strategies

It's not that cooking for one is wholly different from any other kind of cooking. In certain respects, however, a different mindset can be helpful. Some general guidelines to keep in mind.

Go for quality

Choosing the best ingredients is the first and most crucial step toward a wonderful meal. Ripe seasonal produce, organic milk, fine cheeses, fish that looks and smells really fresh—these are the kind of foods you want. They may not cost any more than lesser foods, but if they do, it's probably not going to break the bank. After all, you're just buying enough for yourself.

Spice up your cooking

Buy dried herbs and spices in small quantities, and prolong their life by storing them, tightly sealed, in a dark, cool cupboard. Paprika and other chiles should go in the freezer. Multi-ingredient blends such as garam masala and Italian seasoning can be a smart buy—they're convenient to use, and they eliminate the need to buy spices and herbs you would use only rarely.

Think small when buying perishables

It's easy to become disillusioned with serves-one cooking when faced with the unpleasant task of throwing out spoiled produce you had planned to prepare. The problem is buying too much in the first place. Before you shop, check your calendar and be clear in your mind about how many meals you'll be making in the next few days. Buy only the perishables (fruit, veggies, dairy products) you're sure you can use.

Stock up on staples

Make sure you always have shelf-stable items such as canned beans, couscous, and jarred marinara sauce in your cupboard. At any given time, you should have the makings of at least one spur-of-the-moment meal on hand—for example, olive oil, red pepper flakes, and garlic to make a quick sauce for spaghetti. And don't be afraid to buy condiments and flavor enhancers such as chili paste, soy sauce, and dried mushrooms—they'll keep indefinitely, and they contribute so much to your cooking.

Choose the right markets

Try to patronize supermarkets and other vendors that are sympathetic to the serves-one mentality. Life is just easier if the fish-counter guy will cheerfully wrap up the six scallops you need or cut a tuna steak in half. Buying olives by the ounce at a deli counter or grains from bins in a health food store allows you to fine-tune the quantities of food you take home.

stocking up

These are some foods that are usually in my pantry and refrigerator. Obviously, you don't need all of them to make a good meal for yourself—pick and choose, based on what you like to make and how often you cook.

ANCHOVIES jarred in olive oil, or purchased by the ounce from an Italian deli; use for flavoring sauces; keeps well, refrigerated in olive oil

ASIAN SEASONINGS miso, soy sauce, teriyaki sauce, oyster sauce, instant hon dashi (for making Japanese broth)

BACON (or pancetta—unsmoked Italian bacon) preferably by the ounce, from a deli; can be frozen

BEANS AND LEGUMES (canned and perhaps dried) one or two kinds (e.g., chickpeas, black beans, white beans, lentils)

BREADS fresh bread or sandwich rolls, plus flour tortillas; all keep well in the freezer

BROTH chicken and/or vegetable; preferably organic, aseptically packaged in a box

CHEESE small wedge of Parmigiano-Reggiano, double wrapped in plastic wrap; one or two other cheeses for short-term use

CONDIMENTS e.g., mayonnaise, Dijon mustard, mango chutney, salsa

FRUIT (DRIED) raisins or currants, dried cranberries or cherries

FRUIT (FRESH) lemons and/or limes, plus seasonal fruit for snacking

GRAINS one or two varieties of rice (e.g., basmati, Arborio, jasmine, instant brown rice), bulgur, couscous, quick-cooking polenta and/or stone-ground cornmeal, regular oatmeal, popcorn

HERBS dried oregano, thyme, rosemary, sage, and/or Italian seasoning blend; fresh herbs for short-term use (e.g., basil, dill)

HOT STUFF dried chiles (store in the freezer), Asian chili paste (sambal oelek), Tabasco or other hot pepper sauce; fresh ginger root (refrigerated or frozen to grate as needed)

MUSHROOMS fresh mushrooms such as white button, portabellas, etc., for short-term use; dried mushrooms (e.g., porcini, shiitakes), stored in the freezer

NUTS at least two kinds (e.g., pecans, pine nuts, almonds, walnuts), stored in the freezer

OIL extra-virgin olive oil, refined vegetable oil (e.g., grapeseed, canola), toasted sesame oil

OLIVES imported from the Mediterranean (e.g., kalamata, Gaeta, Sicilian, oil-cured); from a jar or by the ounce, from a deli counter

ONION FAMILY garlic, shallots, onions, scallions (green onions)

PASTA AND NOODLES (DRIED) long (e.g., spaghetti, egg noodles, soba) and short (penne, farfalle)

POTATOES a week's supply (e.g., russet, red-skinned, Yukon)

SALAD MAKINGS greens (can be prewashed) and other veggies; stored in the vegetable compartment

SEAFOOD (CANNED) tuna (oil-packed), salmon, and sardines, if you like them

SPICES salt (preferably kosher or sea salt), black peppercorns, bay leaves, cinnamon, cumin, ground red pepper, crushed red pepper, sesame seeds, seasoning blends (e.g., Southwest seasoning, garam masala)

TOMATO-BASED PRODUCTS good-quality marinara sauce, canned Italian plum tomatoes (diced or whole), sun-dried tomatoes

herbs, etc.

The ingredients singled out here have the potential to lift your meal from ordinary to restaurant quality. Even when you're adding just a little, the flavor comes through.

Fresh herbs

Fresh herbs pose a dilemma, because they are perishable and you usually have to buy more than you can use in a brief period of time. But they add a dimension to some dishes that would be sorely missed if you omitted them.

The ideal solution is to grow a few herbs, and clip just what you need. I have a small plot where I can grow basil, rosemary, sage, thyme, dill, flat-leaf parsley, and mint about half of the year. If you live in a part of the country with a temperate climate, you'll do even better; most herbs are perennials and, as such, will just keep going. Herbs can also be grown in pots, if you have a terrace or sunny windowsill.

Alternatively, buy fresh, aromatic herbs and refrigerate to lengthen their life. Basil and mint do well in a jar partly filled with water, while thyme, dill, and rosemary can be wrapped in damp paper towels.

Use herbs creatively. I never worry about having too much basil, because it's so easy to make pesto with any extra. Mint is also a candidate for pesto—or make a mint julep or mint tea.

Preserve the flavor. Mix chopped herbs with softened butter or olive oil; refrigerate or freeze to use as needed on bread or in a salad dressing.

Lose the guilt. If all else fails: Toss the leftover herb with a clear conscience. If you got one or two good meals out of it, the purchase was worthwhile.

Extra-virgin olive oil

There are olive oils and then there are olive oils. Some you'll find on the supermarket shelf are mass-produced blends that have been chemically manipulated to qualify as extra-virgin oil. They're okay for cooking, but for salads and other foods where the flavor of the oil really matters, an artisanal oil that is 100 percent cold-pressed extra-virgin olive oil is far better. The label may not clarify how it's made, but one taste and you'll know. Rather than buying two grades of olive oil, I'd recommend just getting the good one. For cooking, combine it with a general-purpose vegetable oil.

Wine vinegars

If you're going to have good olive oil, you might as well buy vinegar that measures up. A bottle of traditionally made balsamic vinegar or condimento would be first on my list for enhancing everything from a salad dressing to a fish fillet. I'd also suggest buying a bottle of good-quality white-wine vinegar. As with the olive oil, tasting is the best way to judge quality.

Salt and pepper

I keep fine sea salt in a shaker to season some foods once they're prepared. But mostly I rely on coarse kosher salt in a small covered jar by the stove. Using your fingers to add a pinch or two, you can literally feel how much salt you're adding to your food. When you need more, as when seasoning water for pasta, just dump some into your hand.

As for pepper, once it's ground, the flavor dissipates quickly, so make a habit of using freshly ground black pepper in whatever you're making. Use a refillable pepper mill, or buy peppercorns in a jar fitted with a small grinder.

Wine

No doubt about it, a bottle of wine is sized for serving several people rather than just one. But that's no reason to forgo the pleasure of drinking a glass or two of wine with a meal. You can purchase a vacuum-sealing wine stopper that will help keep the contents of a bottle fresh for several days once it's been opened, or take a look at "splits," the demi-bottles sold by many wine stores. When you have a partially used bottle of wine, consider making one of the recipes in *Serves One* calling for wine.

Dry white vermouth over ice with a twist of lemon peel is one of my favorite aperitifs. Because it is shelf-stable, vermouth is also very nice to have on hand when a stew or sauce needs a splash of wine; its gentle hints of herbs and spices are a bonus.

tools

No special equipment is needed for serves-one cooking. If you've been cooking for several years, you probably own what you need for preparing small quantities of food. In case you need to acquire some cookware or other tools, however, here are some suggestions.

Knives

The three knives I use all the time are a paring knife, a ten-inch cook's knife for chopping and slicing, and a serrated knife for cutting breads and tomatoes.

Cookware

MEDIUM-SIZE SKILLET (about ten inches in diameter) for sautéing and stir-frying. You can use what is, strictly speaking, a sauté pan with vertical sides, or one with sloping sides. A heavy-duty anodized aluminum skillet could be used both on top of the stove and in the oven. If you're going to have two skillets, consider getting one with a nonstick surface and another made of cast iron; the latter is unparalleled for its browning abilities but may react with acidic foods, so it shouldn't be the only one you own.

SMALL SKILLET (about seven inches across) is just right for tasks such as making an omelet or toasting a few nuts.

SMALL SAUCEPAN very handy for cooking or reheating single servings; 1 + 1/2 quarts is a good size, and it should have a cover. I have one that's roughly twice as broad as it is deep and find it useful for making one-pot meals that start with sautéing. You could also use a small flat-bottom wok as a dual-purpose skillet and saucepan.

MEDIUM-SIZE SAUCEPAN holding about four quarts is what you'll need for cooking pasta and making small batches of soup.

Appliances

TOASTER OVEN is at the top of my list. It's great for serves-one cooking, because it heats up much faster than a conventional oven, and the proportions are a fit for the small amount you're making. Obviously, you can make a toasted sandwich in it or reheat foods like pizza that would sog out or turn tough in a microwave. But you can also cook a pizza, foil-wrapped salmon, or other single-serving dish.

MICROWAVE OVEN You can trust a microwave oven to thaw and reheat foods efficiently and to perform small chores like melting butter. It also does a good job of cooking some vegetables, "poaching" a fish or chicken fillet, and cooking rice. But you can use a burner on your stove to do the same thing, so I would not consider this to be an essential piece of kitchen equipment for the serves-one cook.

BLENDER Great for making pureed soups, smoothies, and, when you're in the mood, a frozen daiquiri.

FOOD PROCESSOR Personally, I couldn't do without a food processor—in fact, it's my favorite piece of kitchen equipment. I use it for chopping ingredients; pureeing pesto, hummus, and other mixtures too thick for a blender to handle; mixing a batch of cookie batter; and a million other things. Food processors are very durable—I just replaced my Cuisinart after twenty-five years of faithful service and chose a standard eleven-cup model.

GRILLS If you have a terrace or backyard, get an outdoor grill of some sort. If you don't mind making a fire, you get the best flavor from a charcoal grill, which could be just a small hibachi. For convenience, you can't beat a gas grill, which fires up in no time flat. Countertop grills have many fans, but I am not among them. The smallest is a good size for small-scale cooking, but I don't find it to be more convenient or significantly speedier than stovetop cooking.

More Tools

You'll also need the following basic kitchenware and utensils:

SMALL ROASTING PAN

RIMMED BAKING SHEET

COLANDER

SMALL STRAINER

MEASURING CUPS AND SPOONS

WOODEN SPOON

HEATPROOF SPATULA

PAIR OF PINCER-TYPE TONGS

VEGETABLE PEELER

WHISK

SMALL CHEESE GRATER OR MICROPLANE

INSTANT-READ THERMOMETER

PEPPER MILL

Other Handy Supplies

SCALE A digital scale is an aid not only in weighing ingredients, but, if you wish, in tracking portion size.

STORAGE For use in freezing single servings, lay in a supply of recloseable plastic one-quart bags and microwave-safe plastic containers in one- and two-cup sizes. The bags will also be useful for marinating a tuna steak or chicken breast.

salads

Salad Strategies

Crunchy Toppings

Substantial Salads

- Basic Vinaigrette
- Chopped Salad with Deli Turkey and Avocado
- Frisée with Fried Egg and Bacon
- Smoked Trout and Potato Salad
- Chickpea and Tuna Salad
- Warm Spinach, Orzo, and Pistachio Salad

Side Salads

- Roasted Corn and Black Bean Salad
- Tabbouleh
- Greek Salad
- Japanese-Style Marinated Veggies
- Mixed Greens with Seasonal Fruit and Gorgonzola
- Josy's Green Bean and Mushroom Salad

Whether I am making a meal-size extravaganza with all my favorite ingredients or just a little salad to go with something else, I try to start with nice greens. If Boston lettuce at the supermarket looks the freshest and most unblemished, that's what I buy, even if I had planned to buy mixed spring greens.

On that leafy foundation, I can build almost anything. There are some combinations, such as the chopped salad and Greek salad recipes, that I go back to over and over. Other salads are inspired by whatever turns up in the pantry and refrigerator. Raw vegetables, fresh or dried fruit, and nuts or seeds are some obvious candidates. If I run across a few spears of lightly cooked asparagus, the remains of last night's salmon fillet or rice pilaf, or a sautéed chicken breast, I know that my meal preparations are almost complete.

Salad strategies

Choosing greens

● Buy greens in small quantities for quick use. Mixed spring greens (mesclun), sold by the ounce, romaine hearts, and baby Bibb lettuce are well-sized for the single-serving cook.

● When holding power is a priority, choose sturdy greens that will keep for up to a week. Examples: romaine, iceberg, escarole, Belgian endive, radicchio.

● Prewashed greens such as baby spinach are a worthwhile convenience. Mixed salad greens offer variety but will disappoint if the greens are limp or, worse, decomposing when you open the package. Seek out a brand, produce market or, best of all, farmer's market that offers consistently good flavor and quality.

● If you eat a lot of salads, consider creating your own blend by buying two kinds of greens each week. Pair mild-tasting greens like leaf lettuce or Boston lettuce with assertively flavored ones—radicchio or Belgian endive, for example—in a two-to-one ratio.

Cleaning greens

● At home, transfer unwashed greens to a perforated plastic vegetable bag or wrap in paper towels before refrigerating.

● To clean, immerse greens in water; lift, and drain in a colander or salad spinner. Change the water and repeat until no soil is left behind. Drain or spin thoroughly and wrap the greens in paper towels or a clean kitchen towel to absorb the remaining moisture. Cleaned and dried in this way, sturdier greens keep for several days. If the greens are more delicate, clean only the amount you plan to use that day.

● Leave prewashed greens in their package until needed. Once the package has been opened, use the greens within a day or two. To crisp the greens, immerse them briefly in cold water, drain, and dry.

Salad maker's shortcuts

● Fresh mixed greens from a well-maintained supermarket salad may be a good deal. Or, take home a little red cabbage or spinach to toss with the romaine in your refrigerator.

● Tired of finding a limp head of celery or moldy cucumber at the bottom of your vegetable crisper? Try buying problem ingredients by the ounce at a salad bar—chopped, sliced, or shredded.

- Indulge in prepped produce such as shredded carrots and julienned zucchini. They're good not just for salads but for soups and stir-fries as well.

- When you want just a few artichoke hearts, chickpeas, or olives, buy them by the ounce at a deli counter or salad bar.

- If a favorite restaurant or salad bar offers a house dressing that you love, purchase some to take home.

Homemade vinaigrette

By making your own dressing, one portion at a time, you can control the quality and proportions of ingredients and match them to the particular salad you are making.

Making a basic vinaigrette is one of those kitchen tasks that can be done more quickly than described. One method is to add each ingredient to the salad separately. After doing it a few times, you'll be able to dress a salad by look and feel, not by measuring. The other way is to mix the dressing, then add it to the salad. Even easier: Whisk together the ingredients in the bottom of the bowl, then add the salad ingredients and toss.

Using a bowl with a capacity twice the volume of your salad makes it easier to toss.

You can vary the vinaigrette through your choice of oil and vinegar.

Other simple ways to add flavor to a single-portion salad:

- Rub a crushed garlic clove over the salad plate, or combine it in a jar with prepared dressing and shake.

- Sprinkle the salad with fresh herbs such as chopped parsley or chives.

- Add bits of a flavorful cheese, such as Gorgonzola, feta, or aged goat cheese.

Buying a salad dressing

When choosing a prepared dressing, be sure to read the nutritional information on the label. Frankly, I often find a long list of additives I'd rather do without. Some things to look for:

- Check the type of oil in the dressing. Olive oil and polyunsaturated oils such as safflower, canola, and soybean are preferable to partially hydrogenated oils or highly saturated oils such as palm or coconut.

- Choose a dressing free of artificial flavors, coloring, and thickeners. Some all-natural dressings are made with organic ingredients.

Crunchy toppings

Crumbled bacon

Fry 1 bacon strip in a small skillet over medium heat until crisp; drain on a paper towel and crumble.

Croutons

Cut any hearty, European-style bread (preferably stale) into cubes, leaving the crusts on. If the bread cubes are soft or moist, heat them on the lowest setting in a toaster oven or a small skillet until they feel dry.

If the bread has a lot of personality, the croutons may taste fine as they are. Otherwise, flavor them as follows:

Remove the bread cubes from the pan. Add a little extra-virgin olive oil and a clove or two of crushed garlic to the pan and cook over medium heat until the garlic turns golden.

Remove the garlic and return the croutons to the pan. Sprinkle with dried thyme, oregano, rosemary, or a seasoning blend.

Cook the cubes, turning them occasionally and checking often to prevent burning. Remove from the heat when they are crisp and have turned golden.

Toasted nuts and seeds

Roasted, salted pistachios, spicy almonds, toasted sesame seeds—these are just a few of the store-bought nuts and seeds to consider as salad toppings.

Alternatively, toast pecans, walnuts, or almonds over medium-low heat in a small skillet or in a 300°F oven for 10 to 15 minutes, until crisp. Sesame and sunflower seeds take less time, about 5 minutes. To deepen the flavor of nuts and seeds, coat them with a little vegetable oil and salt before toasting.

Basic Vinaigrette

One salad may need a little more or a little less dressing than another, and personal tastes can vary. Find a formula that suits you, using this recipe for one portion to get started.

1 tablespoon extra-virgin olive oil
1 teaspoon red or white wine vinegar or balsamic vinegar
Large pinch salt
Freshly ground black pepper, to taste

Ad Hoc Method: Place the greens in a large bowl, sprinkle with the oil, and toss the salad. Sprinkle with the vinegar, and toss again. Add the salt and pepper, and give the salad a final toss.

Premixed Method: Combine oil, vinegar, salt, and pepper in a small jar. Cover and shake vigorously. Drizzle the dressing over the salad and toss.

Variations

—Mustard: Add 1/4 teaspoon coarse or smooth Dijon mustard.

—Citrus: Substitute 1 to 2 teaspoons lemon or lime juice for the vinegar.

Fettuccine with Smoked Salmon and Peas recipe on page **77**

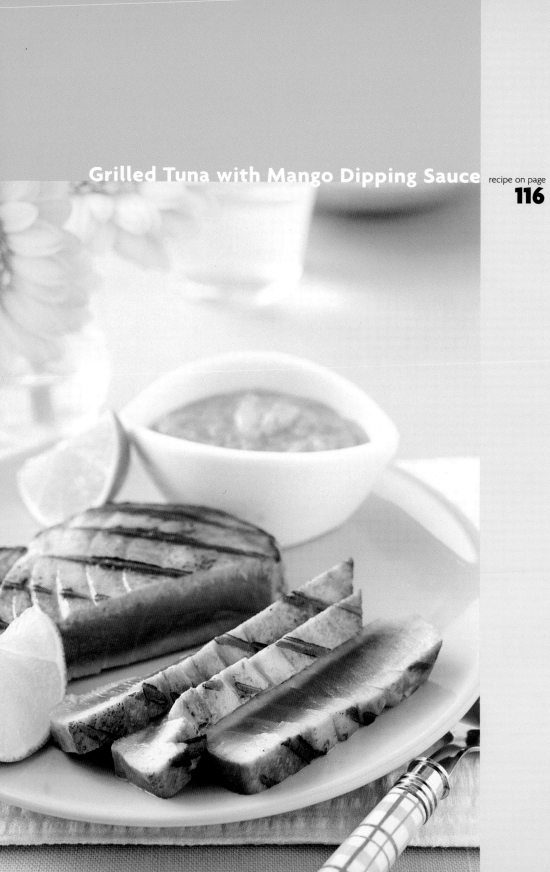

Grilled Tuna with Mango Dipping Sauce recipe on page **116**

Chicken and Baby Bok Choy Stir Fry recipe on page **98**

Grilled Pizza with Brie and Arugula recipe on page
170

Sizzling Shrimp with Garlic recipe on page
121

Warm Spinach, Orzo, and Pistachio Salad recipe on page **37**

Grilled Lamb Chops recipe on page **102**

Soothing Tortellini-Broccolini Soup recipe on page **52**

Chopped Salad with Deli Turkey and Avocado

The idea with a chopped salad is to cut everything fairly small, so you can enjoy all of the flavors, textures, and colors in each bite. Other vegetables that could be added or substituted: radishes, summer squash, celery, and artichoke hearts.

2 ounces deli roast turkey sliced 1/4-inch thick

2 tablespoons store-bought Caesar dressing (such as Newman's Own) or homemade Mustard Vinaigrette (page 32)

2 tablespoons crumbled mild blue cheese (such as Maytag)

1 + 1/2 cups thinly shredded romaine lettuce or romaine heart

1/4 cup chopped or diced tomato

1/4 cup chopped or diced yellow or green bell pepper

2 tablespoons chopped onion or scallions

1/4 cup diced Hass avocado

1 Dice the turkey (makes about 1/3 cup). In the bottom of a bowl large enough for the salad, mix the dressing with the blue cheese.

2 Add the romaine, turkey, tomato, bell pepper, onion, and avocado. Toss with the dressing.

Cook's Note

Cover the rest of the avocado with plastic wrap and refrigerate for up to 2 days. Use it in another salad or on a sandwich, or make a quick guacamole by mashing the avocado with a little salsa, salt, and lime juice.

MAKES 1 SERVING
PREP: 10 MINUTES
COOK: 12 MINUTES

Frisée with Fried Egg and Bacon

Stylish salads like this one are a staple on bistro and brasserie menus, and it's easy to see why. The homey comforts of egg and bacon are bedded down on bitter greens with a piquant dressing.

2 teaspoons plus 1 teaspoon olive oil

1 teaspoon white wine vinegar

1/4 teaspoon Dijon mustard

Salt and freshly ground black pepper

1 + 1/2 cups torn frisée (baby chicory)

1 slice bacon or pancetta (unsmoked Italian bacon)

1 egg

Grape tomatoes or tomato wedges

2 tablespoons crumbled Roquefort or other blue cheese (optional)

1 Combine 2 teaspoons olive oil, the vinegar, mustard, a pinch of salt, and dash of pepper in a medium bowl. Add the frisée and toss. Transfer to a shallow soup/pasta bowl.

2 Lay the bacon strip in a small skillet and, over medium heat, cook on both sides until crisp, about 8 minutes. Drain on a paper towel. Discard the bacon grease and wipe the skillet clean with a paper towel.

3 Heat the remaining 1 teaspoon olive oil in the same skillet. Crack the eggshell, letting the egg slide into the pan. Sprinkle lightly with salt and pepper. Cook until the white of the egg turns opaque but the yolk is still soft, about 3 minutes.

4 Transfer the egg with a spatula onto the dressed greens. Crumble the bacon on top. Arrange the tomatoes and Roquefort (if using) around the egg.

Smoked Trout and Potato Salad

2–3 fingerling or small red potatoes, cut into wedges (about 3/4 cup)

1 tablespoon extra-virgin olive oil

1–2 teaspoons red wine vinegar or sherry vinegar

1/4 teaspoon Dijon mustard

1/4 teaspoon salt

1 pinch freshly ground black pepper

1 + 1/2 cups torn Boston or leaf lettuce

2 ounces smoked trout (about 1/2 cup)

1 slice sweet onion

3–4 grape or cherry tomatoes, halved

1 hard-cooked egg, cut in wedges (optional)

1 Place the potatoes and 1/4 cup water in a microwave-safe dish. Cover loosely with plastic wrap and microwave on high until tender, about 3 minutes.

2 Meanwhile, combine the olive oil, vinegar, mustard, salt, and pepper in a small jar; cover and shake. In a medium bowl, toss the lettuce with half of the dressing. Scoop the greens onto a dinner plate.

3 Drain the potatoes and, in the same bowl, gently combine with the remainder of the dressing. Spoon the potatoes onto the greens.

4 With your fingers, separate trout flesh from skin and break into pieces. Arrange on the salad, along with the onion, tomatoes, and hard-cooked egg (if using).

Chickpea and Tuna Salad

Even when the larder is fairly bare, I usually have the ingredients for this salad on hand, and it's nice to know I can whip up a well-balanced meal in a few minutes. Eat it with pita triangles or sourdough bread, if you like.

1 cup chickpeas (half of a 19-ounce can), drained and rinsed

1 (3-ounce) can oil-packed tuna (preferably from Spain or Italy), drained

1 scallion, including most of the green part, chopped

2 tablespoons chopped red bell pepper

3 imported black olives, such as Kalamata or niçoise, pitted and sliced

1 + 1/2 tablespoons extra-virgin olive oil

1 tablespoon fresh lemon juice

Salt

Crushed red pepper or freshly ground black pepper

Mixed salad greens

1 Combine the chickpeas, tuna, scallion, bell pepper, olives, olive oil, and lemon juice in a bowl. Season to taste with the salt and crushed red pepper.

2 Line a plate or shallow bowl with salad greens, and spoon the chickpea-tuna salad on top.

MAKES 1 GENEROUS SERVING (2 TO 2 + 1/2 CUPS)
PREP: 10 MINUTES
COOK: 10 MINUTES

Warm Spinach, Orzo, and Pistachio Salad

My daughter Kate acquired this recipe from a college friend, and it's become one of our favorites. It's wonderfully flexible—you can go heavy on the spinach or, if you like, cut back and add a little more orzo. The salad tastes good right away, while still warm, but if you have some left over, save it as tomorrow's treat.

1/4 teaspoon salt, plus a large pinch

1/4 cup orzo (rice-shaped pasta)

2 tablespoons crumbled feta cheese

2 teaspoons extra-virgin olive oil

2 teaspoons balsamic vinegar

Freshly ground black pepper

1 + 1/2 cups baby spinach leaves

2 tablespoons chopped red onion

1 heaping tablespoon roasted pistachios

1 In a small saucepan, combine 2 cups water with 1/4 teaspoon salt. Bring to a boil over medium-high heat. Add the orzo and cook until al dente, about 7 minutes.

2 Meanwhile, combine the feta, olive oil, vinegar, a large pinch of salt, and pepper to taste in a medium bowl.

3 Drain the orzo through a strainer (not a colander—some of the orzo may escape through the holes!) and add to the bowl. Gently stir to coat the orzo with the dressing. Add the spinach, onion, and pistachios, and toss once more.

Roasted Corn and Black Bean Salad

You could use frozen corn for this recipe but, believe me, the two minutes it takes to cut the kernels off fresh corn is worth it. If it's summer, buy locally grown corn. The rest of the year, supersweet corn grown in the South is widely available, and the quality is excellent.

1 ear fresh corn, husked

2 teaspoons vegetable or olive oil

Pinch ground red pepper

1 cup canned black beans, drained and rinsed

1 large radish, halved and thinly sliced

2 tablespoons chopped sweet onion

1 packed tablespoon chopped cilantro leaves

1 tablespoon fresh lime juice

1/4 teaspoon salt, or to taste

1 Holding the corn upright on a cutting board, cut off the kernels with a sharp knife.

2 Heat the oil in a small skillet over medium-high heat. Add the corn and ground red pepper. Cook, stirring often, until some of the kernels are browned, about 5 minutes. If the corn starts to char, the heat's too high; reduce it to medium.

3 Scrape the corn out of the pan into a shallow soup/pasta bowl. Stir in the beans, radish, onion, cilantro, lime juice, and salt.

Tabbouleh

This refreshing grain salad is made in the traditional way, with lots of fresh parsley—which can count as your green vegetable. Serve it with grilled chicken or steak or, for a complete meal in itself, just add cooked baby shrimp.

1/2 cup bulghur wheat

3/4 cup chopped tomato

1/2 cup chopped fresh flat-leaf parsley

2 tablespoons chopped fresh mint (optional)

1 scallion, including most of the green part, chopped

2 tablespoons extra-virgin olive oil

2 tablespoons fresh lemon juice

1/4 teaspoon salt, or to taste

1 Place the bulghur in a small bowl and pour 1/2 cup boiling water over it. Cover and set aside until the bulghur absorbs the water, about 15 minutes. Fluff gently with a fork.

2 Mix in the tomato, parsley, mint (if using), scallion, olive oil, lemon juice, and salt. Let stand at least 30 minutes for flavors to blend.

Cook's Note

Try spooning tabbouleh into a pita pocket, or add a little to hot tomato soup or chicken broth.

Greek Salad

This is a worthy mate for a steak or lamb chops (page 102).

1 small tomato or 6 grape or cherry tomatoes

1/2 small cucumber, peeled

2 torn romaine lettuce leaves

3–4 imported black olives, such as Kalamata or niçoise, pitted and slivered (see Note)

2 tablespoons crumbled feta cheese

2 teaspoons extra-virgin olive oil

2 teaspoons lemon juice

1 large pinch dried oregano

Salt and freshly ground black pepper, to taste

1 Cut the tomato into bite-size pieces, or halve the grape tomatoes. Cut the cucumber lengthwise in half and, if you like, scrape out the seeds with a spoon; cut crosswise in slices.

2 On a salad plate or in a shallow bowl, combine the tomato, cucumber, romaine, olives, and feta cheese. Sprinkle the olive oil, lemon juice, oregano, and salt and pepper over the salad and mix gently.

Cook's Note

Buy pitted olives, sold by the ounce in many delis.

Japanese-Style Marinated Veggies

This refreshing and virtually fat-free salad belongs to the Japanese category of foods known as sunomono ("vinegared things"). It's especially good with fish or fried softshell crab (page 123).

1/4 cucumber, peeled and thinly sliced (about 1/3 cup)

3 thinly sliced radishes or 3 thin slices tomato

1 thin slice onion

1 tablespoon unseasoned rice vinegar

1/4 teaspoon sugar

1/4 teaspoon salt

1 On a serving plate, layer the cucumber, radishes, and onion.

2 In a small dish, combine the rice vinegar, sugar, and salt. Spoon the dressing over the vegetables. Let stand 10 minutes or up to 12 hours.

Cook's Note

For the dressing, you can use 2 tablespoons seasoned rice vinegar, which already contains sugar and salt, and skip the additional sugar and salt.

MAKES 1 SERVING
PREP: 10 MINUTES

Mixed Greens with Seasonal Fruit and Gorgonzola

Nectarines and blueberries are in season at the same time, so why not include both in this delightful summer salad? In fall and winter, use apple, pear, mango, papaya, or persimmon. Strawberries or raspberries would be the right choice in spring. Serve with roast chicken, salmon, or a pork chop.

1 tablespoon extra-virgin olive oil

1 teaspoon white wine vinegar

1 teaspoon honey

Salt and freshly ground black pepper, to taste

1 + 1/2 cups microgreens (tiny baby salad greens) or other mixed greens

1/2 nectarine or peach, sliced

1/4 cup blueberries

1 ounce aged Gorgonzola, crumbled (about 1/4 cup)

1 With a fork, whisk together the olive oil, vinegar, honey, and salt and pepper in a small bowl.

2 Place the greens in a bowl. Toss with half of the dressing. Transfer to a dinner plate.

3 In the same bowl, gently mix the nectarine slices and blueberries with the rest of the dressing. Top the greens with the fruit and distribute the Gorgonzola bits over the salad.

MAKES 1 SERVING
PREP: 15 MINUTES
COOK: 8 MINUTES

Josy's Green Bean and Mushroom Salad

Josyane Colwell, owner of Le Moulin in Irvington, New York, says her delightful salad is ideal for a French-style picnic. You can purchase everything else: a thick slice of baked ham or pâté from a good deli, a ripe pear or melon slice (ideally, the small, striped kind called cavillon) and perhaps a little Brie or Roquefort for dessert. Add a crusty roll, a pleasing wine and you have the makings of a fresh-air feast—even if it takes place on your own terrace or by an open window.

Pinch salt, plus more for bean water

1/3 pound green beans or haricots verts, ends trimmed (about 1 + 1/2 cups)

1 + 1/2 tablespoons extra-virgin olive oil

1 tablespoon cider or white wine vinegar

1/8 teaspoon grainy Dijon mustard

Freshly ground black pepper, to taste

3 medium white mushrooms, sliced

1 ounce semisoft pecorino or Gruyère cheese, cut into matchsticks

2 tablespoons roughly chopped red onion

1 Bring a pot of water to a boil; add salt. Add the beans and boil until tender but still crisp, 2 to 3 minutes; drain.

2 Meanwhile, combine the oil, vinegar, mustard, salt, and pepper in a small bowl. Add the beans, mushrooms, cheese, and onion, and mix gently.

soups

Broth Basics

Soup for the Freezer

Good Beginnings

- Roasted Vegetable Stock
- Your Own Chicken Broth

One or Two Servings

- Gingery Carrot and Celery Soup
- Soothing Tortellini-Broccolini Soup
- Miso Soup in a Mug
- Avocado-Cucumber Soup
- Kale and Kielbasa Soup
- Soba Noodles and Shrimp in Broth
- Cabbage and Cheese Soup
- Creamy Tomato Soup

Soup by the Batch

- Hearty Potato Soup
- Lemony Lentil Soup
- Beef, Barley, and Mushroom Soup

Almost Instant Soups

Homemade soup sounds a little daunting, like something that should not be attempted unless you have all day to watch it simmer. In fact, many tasty soups can be whipped up so quickly that making just one or two servings isn't a big deal.

Of course, some soups are best made in larger batches. And there's nothing wrong with having a cache of homemade soup tucked away in your refrigerator or freezer. When you come home exhausted, it's nice to dip out a bowlful or thaw a single serving. These recipes make a fairly small quantity—two or three quarts—so you won't tire of the soup before it's gone.

Your meal in a bowl can be made entirely from fresh ingredients and your own homemade broth. Or, you can get good results by combining fresh ingredients with frozen, dried, or canned ingredients. When you're short on time, turn to the Almost-Instant Soups suggestions at the end of the chapter.

You can use any small or medium saucepan to make the single-portion soups. To make soup by the batch, you will need a larger saucepan—possibly the same one you use to cook pasta. Ideally, the bottom of your soup pot should be heavy, to prevent burning, and fairly broad, for recipes that begin with sautéing some ingredients.

Soup savvy

Broth basics

Whether you choose canned broth, bouillon cubes, or a concentrate, choose a superior product. Read the label carefully, to make sure the product does not contain hydrogenated oil, MSG, glutens, and other ingredients you may not welcome. Be sure to compare samples of several products (in diluted form) before settling on a favorite; some may taste mainly of salt, while others will have a full-bodied flavor closer to that of homemade broth. If you can find broth made from organic ingredients, all the better.

I often use so-called "natural" chicken and vegetable stocks made by Kitchen Basics. They come in aseptic packaging, with a recloseable lid, so I don't have to use it all at once.

A high-quality concentrate is also convenient for single-portion cooking. The paste can be spooned from the jar and diluted with hot water to make the quantity needed, and it keeps indefinitely in the refrigerator. I've used chicken and mushroom bases called Better than Bouillon, available in some supermarkets.

At least once in a while, consider making your own broth. It's a simple thing to do, and the flavor really is superior. Make a big batch, freeze it in 1- and 2-cup containers, and you'll be well stocked (pardon the pun) for a long time.

Soup for the freezer

● Ladle 2 cups cooked soup into each plastic container. Seal securely and label with the name of the soup and the date.

● When reusing flimsy deli or cottage cheese containers, enclose each one in a recloseable plastic freezer bag for extra protection. For sturdy, microwaveable containers, such as Rubbermaid or Tupperware, stack as is, in the freezer.

● Thaw soups in the refrigerator or microwave. Or, leave at room temperature just long enough for the soup to loosen from the sides; then heat in a microwave or over a burner.

MAKES 2 QUARTS
PREP: 10 MINUTES
COOK: 40 MINUTES

Roasted Vegetable Stock

This vegetable essence has a golden-brown color and grounded flavor that comes from browning the vegetables first and including mushrooms in the mix. And, honestly, it's so simple to make. I peel the onion for easier browning but not the other vegetables. No need to simmer this broth for hours—30 minutes will do.

1 tablespoon olive oil or other vegetable oil

1 medium onion, roughly chopped

2 medium carrots, roughly chopped

1 celery rib, roughly chopped

2 unpeeled cloves garlic, lightly crushed

2 cups quartered mushrooms, or trimmings (see Note)

1 bay leaf

1 teaspoon salt

1/2 teaspoon peppercorns

1 Heat the oil over medium-high heat in a large saucepan with a fairly broad bottom. Add the onion, carrots, celery, and garlic. Cook, stirring often, until the vegetables soften and start to brown, about 10 minutes.

2 Stir in the mushrooms and bay leaf. Cook, stirring 5 minutes longer. Meanwhile, bring 2 + 1/2 quarts water to a boil. Add the water to the vegetable mixture, along with the salt and peppercorns.

3 When the water returns to a boil, reduce the heat so that the ingredients cook at a brisk simmer. Cook, partly covered, for about 30 minutes. Let cool.

4 Strain the broth into a bowl or other container. Store the amount that you expect to use within a week in the refrigerator and freeze the rest in 1- or 2-cup plastic containers.

SOUPS

Cook's Notes

—Save trimmings such as mushroom stem ends and portabella and shiitake stems—plus mushrooms you're pretty sure you won't get around to using—in a recloseable plastic bag in your freezer. Freezing changes the texture of mushrooms but not the flavor; because they're strained out, the texture doesn't matter.

—Try adding parsley leaves and/or stems, other fresh herbs such as chives or thyme, or virtually anything in the onion family (scallions, leeks, etc.).

—Some veggies that don't work in broth are asparagus, radishes, and vegetables in the cabbage family (such as broccoli and cauliflower).

MAKES 3 QUARTS
PREP: 15 MINUTES
COOK: 1–2 HOURS

Your Own Chicken Broth

The old-fashioned stewing chicken has vanished from supermarkets and butcher shops, and chicken necks and backs can be hard to find, too. Fortunately, broth can be made successfully with chicken or turkey wings, which are sold separately in most supermarkets.

2 + 1/2 pounds chicken or turkey wings

2 carrots, trimmed and cut into chunks

1 medium onion, quartered

1 celery rib, trimmed and cut into chunks

1–2 bay leaves

1 tablespoon salt (optional) (see Note)

1/2 teaspoon peppercorns

1 Rinse the chicken or turkey wings and pile them in the bottom of a large saucepan or stockpot. Add the carrots, onion, celery, bay leaf, salt (if using), and peppercorns, and cover with water. Bring the mixture to a boil. Reduce the heat to low.

2 Simmer the broth, partly covered, for 1 to 2 hours, skimming any scum that rises to the top. Allow the broth to cool slightly, and strain through a fine-mesh strainer into a bowl or other container; cover and refrigerate until cold.

3 Skim the congealed fat off the top of the chilled broth. Return the amount of broth that you expect to use within a week to the refrigerator and freeze the rest in 1- or 2-cup plastic containers.

Cook's Note

I usually omit the salt, because it frees me to use the broth as an ingredient in any recipe, seasoning as appropriate. If you prefer a fully seasoned broth, add the salt.

Gingery Carrot and Celery Soup

This soup is equally delicious hot or cold.

2 small carrots, peeled and chopped (about 1 + 1/2 cups)

1/2 cup chopped celery

2 teaspoons grated or chopped ginger root

1 teaspoon salt, or to taste

2 tablespoons couscous

1/4 teaspoon freshly ground black or white pepper

1 In a medium saucepan, combine the carrots, celery, ginger, and salt; cover with water. Bring the mixture to a boil. Reduce the heat and simmer, partly covered, until the carrots are tender, about 10 minutes.

2 Stir in the couscous and the pepper, and cook 5 minutes longer. Remove from the burner and allow to cool slightly.

3 Transfer the mixture to a blender or food processor. Blend or process until smooth. Taste and add more salt if needed.

Variation

Creamy Carrot Soup: After pureeing the soup, return it to the saucepan and stir in 1/4 cup half-and-half. Reheat over low heat. Alternatively, if the soup is to be eaten cold, add up to 1/2 cup plain yogurt.

SOUPS

Soothing Tortellini-Broccolini Soup

Redolent of garlic, this soup is especially comforting when you're feeling under the weather.

1 clove garlic

1 + 1/2 cups canned or homemade chicken broth (page 50) (see Note)

1/2 cup fresh or frozen cheese or meat tortellini

1/2 cup chopped broccolini or broccoli crown (see Note)

1/4 cup thin carrot slices

Salt and freshly ground black pepper

Grated Parmigiano-Reggiano or Pecorino Romano cheese (optional)

1 Thinly slice the garlic clove lengthwise, then cut the slices in slivers. Combine the broth with the garlic in a small saucepan. Over high heat, bring to a boil. Reduce the heat to medium and simmer 5 minutes.

2 Add the tortellini, broccolini, and carrot, and cook a few minutes longer, until the vegetables are tender. Season to taste with salt and pepper. Sprinkle with cheese if you like.

Cook's Notes

—If using canned broth, replace 1/2 cup of the broth with water.

—Broccolini, a hybrid of broccoli and Chinese kale, comes in small bunches, ideal for small-scale cooking.

MAKES 1 SERVING
PREP: 5 MINUTES
COOK: 5 MINUTES

Miso Soup in a Mug

Granted, three of the five ingredients in this recipe could be considered exotic, but in Japan they're staples. They keep indefinitely, ready to help you brew up a steaming mug of miso soup in hardly any time.

2 teaspoons miso (see Note)

3/4 cup canned or homemade chicken broth (page 50) or vegetable broth (page 48)

1/4 teaspoon instant dashi (optional) (see Note)

1/4 teaspoon mirin (see Note)

1 teaspoon thinly sliced scallion

1 In a large mug or soup bowl, use a fork to whisk the miso with 2 tablespoons water until well blended.

2 Combine the broth with 1/2 cup water in a small saucepan, and bring to a boil. Remove from the heat, and stir in the dashi (if using), mirin, and scallion. Add any optional ingredients. Pour into the mug, and stir again.

Cook's Note

Red or white miso, the fermented soy paste that can be transformed so easily into a delectable soup, is available from Asian and other specialty stores. There, in powdered form, you'll also find instant dashi (the mixture of kelp and bonito flakes that adds that "je ne sais quoi" to Japanese broth) and mirin (sweet rice wine).

Optional Add-Ins

1/4 cup diced tofu, 1 thinly sliced shiitake or white mushroom cap, 1/4 cup chopped watercress leaves or thinly sliced baby bok choy

Avocado-Cucumber Soup

Not only is this creamy though creamless soup vegetarian, but it's made entirely from raw ingredients.

1 Hass avocado

1 cup peeled, seeded, chopped cucumber

2 tomatillos, quartered

1/4 cup chopped onion

1 small serrano or jalapeño chile, halved lengthwise, stemmed, and seeded

1 teaspoon salt

2 teaspoons chopped cilantro (optional)

1 Run a knife lengthwise around the avocado and twist to separate the halves. Lightly strike the pit with a knife blade and twist to remove. Score the flesh with a knife and scoop it out with a spoon.

2 In a blender or food processor, combine the avocado, cucumber, tomatillos, onion, chile, and salt. Add 1 cup water. Blend until the mixture is pureed, adding more water if necessary for a soupy consistency. Chill well. Sprinkle with the cilantro, if using.

Cook's Note

Even easier, omit the tomatillos and chile. After pureeing the mixture, add prepared green salsa to taste; blend briefly.

Kale and Kielbasa Soup

Everything goes into the soup pot at once, and within the hour you're ready to eat.

4 + 1/2 cups canned or homemade chicken broth (page 50)
2–3 kale leaves, shredded
1/2 cup chopped onion
1/2 cup diced carrot
1/2 cup sliced celery
1/2 cup cubed kielbasa (Polish sausage)
1 teaspoon chopped garlic
Salt and freshly ground black pepper, to taste

1 Combine the chicken broth, kale, onion, carrot, celery, kielbasa, and garlic in a medium saucepan. Over high heat, bring to a boil.

2 Reduce the heat to medium-low. Simmer the soup, partly covered, until the vegetables are tender, about 30 minutes. Season with salt and pepper.

Soba Noodles and Shrimp in Broth

Japanese buckwheat noodles, heated in a fragrant broth, make a nourishing soup.

1 tablespoon soy sauce

2 teaspoons mirin (Japanese sweet rice wine)

6 medium shelled shrimp

1/4 cup thinly sliced white mushrooms or shiitake caps

1/8 teaspoon instant dashi granules (see Note)

2 ounces dried soba noodles (see Note)

8 snow peas or sugar snap peas, cut diagonally in half

1 tablespoon chopped scallion, including some of the green part

1 In a small saucepan, combine the soy sauce and mirin with 2/3 cup water. Bring to a boil. Add the shrimp and mushrooms, and cook just until the shrimp turn pink, about 30 seconds; remove the shrimp with a slotted spoon and set aside. Reduce the heat to low, and stir the dashi granules into the broth.

2 In a medium saucepan, bring 1 quart water to a boil. Add the soba noodles and snow peas. Boil until the noodles are tender but slightly firm, about 1 minute. Drain and transfer the noodles and snow peas to a shallow soup bowl. Scatter the shrimp over the noodles and pour the warm broth on top. Sprinkle with chopped scallion.

Cook's Note

Look for soba (buckwheat noodles) and instant hon-dashi (dried ground bonito and other seasonings) in specialty stores that sell Asian foods; bottled dashi broth can also be used. If you cannot find these products, substitute vermicelli or ramen noodles for soba and chicken stock for diluted dashi.

MAKES 2 SERVINGS
PREP: 10 MINUTES
COOK: 30 MINUTES

Cabbage and Cheese Soup

2 teaspoons butter

1/2 cup thinly sliced onion

1 cup cole slaw mix

1 cup diced red-skinned potato

2 cups canned or homemade chicken broth (page 50) or vegetable broth (page 48)

1/8–1/4 teaspoon sweet or hot paprika (see Note)

1/2 cup sliced or diced fully cooked sausage, such as Spanish chorizo (optional)

Salt

1 slice Gruyère cheese (per serving), cut into small pieces

1 slice bread (per serving) from a baguette or country loaf, cut into cubes

1 Melt the butter in a medium saucepan over medium heat. Sauté the onion for a few minutes, stirring, until tender.

2 Add the cole slaw mix, potato, broth, paprika, and 2 cups water. Bring to a boil. Reduce heat and simmer the soup, partly covered, until the potato is tender, about 20 minutes. Add the chorizo (if using) 5 minutes before the soup finishes cooking. Taste and add salt if needed.

3 Scatter the Gruyère and bread on the bottom of a shallow soup/pasta bowl. Spoon half the soup on top. Refrigerate or freeze the other serving.

Cook's Note

Keep your eyes open for smoked Spanish paprika or Hungarian paprika, which have more interesting flavors than the ordinary kind.

MAKES 2 SERVINGS
PREP: 10 MINUTES
COOK: 20 MINUTES

Creamy Tomato Soup

On its own or with a toasted ham and cheese sandwich, this soup is as comforting a supper as you'll find. Small touches such as using leek rather than yellow onion and adding a fresh herb at the end make a large flavor difference.

1 tablespoon butter or olive oil

1/2 cup chopped leek, shallot, or onion

2 teaspoons all-purpose flour

1 (14.5-ounce) can diced tomatoes with basil, garlic, and oregano

1/4–1/3 cup half-and-half

Salt and freshly ground black pepper, to taste

1 tablespoon chopped basil leaves, chives, or dill (optional)

1 Melt the butter in a medium saucepan over medium heat. Add the leek, stirring until coated; cover and cook until soft, about 5 minutes. Check once or twice, and lower the heat if the leek begins to brown.

2 Stir in the flour and cook about 30 seconds. Add the tomatoes and 1 canful of water; bring to a boil. Reduce the heat, partially cover the pan, and simmer for about 5 minutes to blend the flavors.

3 Remove from heat and let the soup cool a few minutes. Transfer to a blender, and blend until smooth. Return the soup to the saucepan and reheat, if necessary, over low heat.

4 Stir in the half-and-half and the fresh herb (if using). Taste and add salt and pepper as necessary.

Hearty Potato Soup

Caraway seeds and browned onions give this potato soup a robust flavor, prompting Dina Ebenstein, a Vienna-born cook who gave me the recipe, to call it a winter soup.

3 tablespoons butter

1 large onion, chopped

3 cups peeled and diced potatoes

1 carrot, peeled and grated

1 teaspoon salt

1 tablespoon caraway seeds

1 cup milk

1/4 cup chopped fresh flat-leaf parsley (optional)

1 Melt the butter in a large saucepan (preferably wide-bottomed) over medium heat. Sauté the onion, stirring often, until golden brown (be careful not to burn it).

2 Add the potatoes, carrot, salt, caraway seeds, and enough water to cover. Bring the mixture to a boil, reduce the heat to medium-low, and simmer until the potatoes are tender. Stir in the milk and parsley (if using) and cook until just hot (do not boil).

Lemony Lentil Soup

My mother-in-law, Helen Lydecker, encountered this soup in Egypt and brought back the recipe to make at home in West Texas. Even my husband, formerly a lentil hater, admits that his mom's soup tastes good.

1 tablespoon vegetable oil

1 medium onion, finely chopped

1/2 pound (1 + 1/3 cups) dried lentils, rinsed

1 small carrot, peeled and chopped

1 small zucchini, peeled and chopped

1/2 teaspoon ground cumin

2 teaspoons salt

1 lemon wedge per serving

1 Heat the oil in a medium saucepan over medium heat. Sauté the onion, stirring often, until well browned but not burned.

2 Add the lentils, carrot, zucchini, cumin, and salt. Add enough water to cover the lentils. Bring the mixture to a boil, reduce the heat to low, and simmer, partly covered, until the lentils and vegetables are tender (check occasionally and add water if necessary). Cool the soup about 10 minutes.

3 Transfer the soup in batches to a blender or food processor, making sure not to fill it more than 2/3 full. Puree until smooth. Return the soup to the saucepan and ladle some into a bowl. Squeeze a lemon wedge over it before eating. Refrigerate or freeze the remainder.

Cook's Note

For an ultra-velvety texture, strain the soup.

Beef, Barley, and Mushroom Soup

Teamed up with hearty ingredients like mushrooms and barley, a little meat goes a long way.

1 tablespoon vegetable oil

1/2 cup finely chopped onion

1/2 cup pearl barley or brown rice

1/8 teaspoon freshly ground black pepper, plus more to taste

2 cups beef broth

1/2 pound chuck steak, sliced into thin (1/4-inch) strips 1 inch long (about 1 + 1/4 cups packed)

2 cups sliced white mushrooms

1/2 cup sliced carrot

Salt

1 Heat the oil in a large saucepan over medium heat. Add the onion, barley, and 1/8 teaspoon pepper. Sauté, stirring often, until the onion is translucent and the barley smells toasty, about 3 minutes. Stir in the broth and 5 cups water.

2 Bring the broth to a boil over high heat. With a large spoon, skim off the scum that rises to the top. Add the beef, mushrooms, and carrot. Reduce the heat to low and simmer the soup, partly covered, until the beef and barley are tender, about 30 minutes. Season to taste with salt and, if needed, more pepper.

SOUPS

Almost instant soups

When you are rushed, prepared soups come in handy. Luckily, there are more choices—canned, frozen, or dried—than there used to be. Sometimes just an extra ingredient or two can make a big difference. These single-serving soups take only minutes to make.

Ramen supreme

Simmer 1 cup frozen stir-fry vegetables and 1/2 package (3 ounces) ramen noodles (discard the flavor packet) in 1 + 1/2 cups chicken or vegetable broth. Sprinkle with soy sauce or mash in a bit of miso.

Lemony beef broth

Add a squirt of lemon juice and a dash of Tabasco to 2 cups hot beef broth. Drink the soup from a mug, floating a few oyster crackers on top.

Black bean soup deluxe

Top canned or reconstituted dried black bean soup with chopped red bell pepper, scallions, and a dollop of sour cream.

Pasta in brodo

Heat 2 cups chicken or vegetable broth combined with a splash of tomato or V-8 juice. Simmer with 1 tablespoon pastine (or a small piece of nested vermicelli, broken into pieces) and 1/2 cup fresh or frozen green beans.

Garlic-ginger chicken broth

Simmer 2 crushed garlic cloves and several slices of ginger root in a mixture of 2 cups chicken broth and 1 cup water for 30 minutes to an hour; strain, and sip from a mug.

Potluck gazpacho

Whirl last night's Greek or Italian salad in the blender, and dilute with tomato juice.

pasta & noodles

Pasta is my favorite fallback meal. Peering into my pantry at its most pitiful, I can usually find some spaghetti and the makings of a sauce. Even when there are other choices, though, a steaming bowl of pasta or other noodles is often what I want. Who could tire of a food capable of so many different incarnations?

The recipes I call comfort pasta are simple, and thus they are the ones I make most often. In a good restaurant, each portion of pasta is mixed with its sauce in a small sauté pan over a burner. At home, too, skillet sauces are great. No need to dirty another container, and the sauce and pasta stay hot while you toss them.

Bowl-ready sauces are prepared and held at room temperature, to be mixed with freshly cooked pasta.

Many sauces are easy to make one portion at a time. But homemade marinara sauce and pesto are another matter. They are so nice to have on hand that you may as well make a batch and save some for the freezer.

Pasta primer

Portion size

Two ounces, the usual single-portion size listed on pasta packages, makes the appropriate amount for a first course. Most of these recipes call for three ounces, based on my hunch that the typical solo diner plans to eat pasta as a main dish. If you want less, adjust the recipe or save some for the next day.

Storage

Dried pasta usually comes in a twelve-ounce or one-pound package. After opening a package of, say, macaroni, seal it (if it's a bag) with a plastic clip or tie, or transfer the contents to a plastic container with a lid. I like to store spaghetti and other long pasta in a tall container made for that purpose.

Measuring

You can weigh your portion or, if you like, measure it—a three-ounce serving consists of approximately one cup of short dried pasta. To simplify portioning, divide a pound of spaghetti into five to eight equal portions, securing each one with a plastic tie or rubber band. Or, learn to gauge a portion of long pasta. Hold a bundle in an upright position; if the ends fit on a quarter, it's a three-ounce serving, more or less.

Fresh pasta

Fresh egg pasta such as tagliatelle or ravioli should be refrigerated and eaten within a few days.

Frozen pasta

Remove only the amount of frozen tortellini, cavatelli, or pierogies you need. Rather than thawing, add the frozen pasta immediately to boiling water.

Cooking pasta

Italians say to use enough water for the pasta to "swim," but you don't need to drown it. Six cups of cold water is plenty for a single serving. For this quantity, add one heaping teaspoon salt. Don't be tempted to leave it out! The salt is needed to season the pasta properly—and most of it drains off with the water.

After bringing the water to a boil, add the pasta all at once, pressing spaghetti and other long pasta with a wooden spoon to submerge it. Stir thoroughly to separate the strands or pieces, and boil the pasta to the al dente stage—tender, but still slightly firm to the bite. The required time ranges from two or three minutes, for some fresh pasta, to twelve minutes for some kinds of dried pasta. The only way to tell for sure is to trap a piece with a slotted spoon or fork and bite into it.

Draining

Don't overdo the draining. You may want to add a little of the cooking water to the sauce (paradoxically, the slightly starchy liquid dilutes the sauce at first but then thickens it a little). This can be accomplished by draining the pasta quickly in a colander and, without waiting for all of the water to go through, turning it into the sauce. Because it's a little easier to scoop out a quarter cup of the water before draining, that's the procedure followed in these recipes.

Saucing

Mix the pasta and sauce thoroughly in a warm skillet or bowl, adding the reserved cooking water if needed. Grate cheese over the pasta just before you eat.

Reheating

The easiest way to reheat pasta is to microwave it, loosely covered, at medium power for about a minute. I think the texture is better, however, when the pasta is reheated, over medium heat, in a skillet. Stir often and add a little water or broth if it seems too dry. Leftover pasta can also be steamed over low heat in a covered saucepan; unless it is well sauced, add a little water to prevent sticking.

About Asian noodles

Maybe you've noticed the stiff white skeins of rice noodles—or transparent cellophane noodles—in the Asian section of your supermarket and wondered what to do with them. Once you discover how easy it is to prepare them, and how wonderfully they absorb flavors, you'll want to create your own variations.

Compared to Italian pasta, Asian noodles have a narrow range of shapes, from thin vermicelli-like noodles to wider ones that resemble fettuccine. But they are made of many different ingredients, including rice, mung beans, soybeans, corn, millet, and wheat.

Asian noodles are cooked in boiling water but—again, unlike Italian pasta—without salt. To judge doneness, taste a noodle. The goal: a cooked noodle that is firm but a little softer than the al dente stage for which we strive with Italian pasta. For many varieties, this takes only a few minutes and, in the case of some, a few seconds.

It's fun to experiment with Asian noodles but confusing because package directions are often lacking or in a language other than English. If you'd like to venture past the handful of recipes here, buy a cookbook such as Corinne Trang's excellent *Essentials of Asian Cuisine*.

These are the Asian noodle varieties that I use most often:

● **Soba:** thin Japanese noodles, light brown in color, that are made of buckwheat; can be eaten hot or cold

● **Dried rice sticks or vermicelli:** sticks or skeins of ultra-thin, very white noodles used in Chinese and Southeast Asian cooking; should be soaked at least 15 minutes in cold water, then boiled for about five seconds

● **Cellophane noodles:** no-carb noodles made of mung beans; prepared in the same way as rice noodles; turn transparent when cooked

● **Wheat noodles:** includes Japanese noodles such as thick udon and thin somen, as well as flat Shanghai noodles; precooked wheat noodles, found in some supermarkets and Asian grocery stores, can be stir-fried

● **Ramen:** thin, flat "instant" egg noodles that have been deep-fried then dried; needs only brief cooking

MAKES 1 SERVING
PREP: 5 MINUTES
COOK: 12 MINUTES

Spaghetti with Butter and Cheese

When you're tired and starving, plain (or practically plain) pasta is just the thing.

1 heaping teaspoon salt
3 ounces spaghetti or spaghettini
1/2 tablespoon butter
2 tablespoons freshly grated Parmigiano-Reggiano cheese
Freshly ground black pepper, to taste
3–4 basil leaves, torn (optional)

1 Combine 6 cups water and the salt in a medium saucepan and bring to a boil over high heat. Add the spaghetti, stirring to submerge and separate the strands. Cook the spaghetti until al dente, about 7 minutes.

2 Drain the pasta, reserving several tablespoons of the cooking water, and return the pasta immediately to the saucepan. Pinch off pieces of butter and add to the pasta. With a fork or pasta spoon, lift and mix the pasta just until the butter melts, coating the strands; add the reserved pasta water, if needed, to moisten the pasta. Stir in the cheese, pepper and, if using, the basil.

Variations

—Add 1 cup steamed or sautéed vegetables (fresh or frozen) to the pasta.

—Substitute 4 ounces (about 1 cup) frozen ravioli, cavatelli, or tortellini for the dried pasta. When the stuffed pasta floats, cook it for 1 additional minute.

Linguine Aglio e Olio

This is another recipe based on ingredients you'd normally have in your kitchen, ready for what Italians call a spaghettata, loosely translated as a "spaghetti pig-out."

1 heaping teaspoon salt

3 ounces linguine or spaghetti

1 tablespoon extra-virgin olive oil

1 small clove garlic, chopped

1 tablespoon finely chopped fresh flat-leaf parsley or scallion

Crushed red pepper

1 Combine 6 cups cold water and the salt in a medium saucepan and bring to a boil over high heat. Add the linguine, stirring to submerge and separate the strands.

2 While the pasta cooks, heat the oil over medium heat in a skillet large enough to hold the pasta. Add the garlic and stir for a minute or so until golden. Remove the skillet from the heat.

3 Drain the spaghetti when it is al dente, reserving a few tablespoons of the pasta water. Turn the pasta into the skillet with the seasoned oil. With a fork or pasta spoon, lift and mix the pasta until coated with the oil, adding the reserved pasta water as needed. Add the parsley and crushed red pepper, to taste, and mix well.

<u>Variation</u>

Linguine with Shrimp and Garlic: Sauté 1/2 cup small, shelled shrimp in the oil before adding the garlic. Or, add the same amount of cooked shrimp to the final mixture.

PASTA & NOODLES

Spaghetti alla Carbonara

This classic pasta dish takes only minutes to make, but it needs to proceed like clockwork, so have all the ingredients prepped before you start cooking. In particular, the pasta must be steaming hot when combined with the yolk mixture so that the egg will cook enough to coat the strands properly.

1 egg yolk

1 tablespoon chopped fresh flat-leaf parsley leaves

2 tablespoons freshly grated Parmigiano-Reggiano cheese, divided

1 heaping teaspoon salt

3 ounces spaghetti or linguine

2 teaspoons butter

1 tablespoon finely chopped shallot or onion

1/2 thick slice pancetta, cut into small pieces

1 tablespoon white wine or vermouth (optional)

1 With a fork, beat the egg yolk in a shallow soup/pasta bowl. Whisk in the parsley and half of the Parmigiano-Reggiano.

2 Combine 6 cups water and the salt in a medium saucepan; bring to a boil over high heat. Add the spaghetti, stirring to submerge and separate the strands.

3 Meanwhile, melt the butter in a small skillet over medium heat. Add the shallot and pancetta and cook, stirring often, until they turn golden but not brown. Add the wine and cook, stirring, until it has almost evaporated. Remove from the heat.

4 When the pasta is al dente, drain and immediately turn it into the bowl with the egg mixture, lifting and turning the strands with a fork until coated. Mix in the shallot-pancetta mixture, and sprinkle with the remaining Parmigiano-Reggiano.

Variation

Omit the parsley and add 1/4 cup fresh or frozen peas to the pasta water during the final 2 minutes of cooking.

Egg Noodles and Cabbage

When I asked my friend Alice Gottlieb how to make egg noodles and cabbage, a dish I had heard of but never eaten, she said, "It's comfort food—there's not really a recipe." Eventually, Alice relented and told me what to do, but she had a point. Once you've made this satisfying and extremely easy meal, you'll never need the recipe again, as long as you remember one rule: The amount of cabbage should be roughly equal in volume to the quantity of egg noodles.

1 tablespoon butter

2 cups cole slaw mix

1 heaping teaspoon salt, plus more to taste

Freshly ground black pepper, to taste

3 ounces broad egg noodles

1 Melt the butter over medium heat in a skillet large enough to hold the cabbage and noodles. Cook the cabbage, stirring occasionally, until the shreds soften and brown around the edges, about 10 minutes (reduce the heat if the cabbage seems in danger of burning). Season with salt and pepper.

2 Meanwhile, bring 6 cups water and 1 heaping teaspoon salt to a boil in a medium saucepan. Add the noodles, stirring to submerge and separate the strands. Cook until al dente, about 4 minutes. Drain, reserving several tablespoons of the cooking water. Add the noodles to the saucepan with the cabbage. Stir until well mixed, adding the water as needed to moisten the pasta.

Pierogies with Sautéed Onions and Mushrooms

Pierogies are pasta half-moons with a filling that usually includes potatoes. Unless you have a Polish grandmother, buy Mrs. T's Pierogies, which are available just about anywhere.

1/2 tablespoon butter

6 thin slices onion

3–4 white mushrooms, thinly sliced

4 frozen potato and cheddar or potato, cheddar, and broccoli pierogies

1–2 teaspoons chopped fresh dill leaves (optional)

Salt and freshly ground black pepper, to taste

1 Melt the butter in a medium skillet over medium-high heat. Add the onion and cook, stirring often, until golden, about 5 minutes. Add the mushrooms and cook a few minutes longer, until they soften and release their liquid.

2 While the onion and mushrooms are cooking, bring 1 quart water to a boil in a medium saucepan. Add the pierogies and cook until they float to the surface, then continue to cook 1 minute longer. If the onion-mushroom mixture seems dry, add enough of the pasta cooking water to create a saucy consistency.

3 Drain the pierogies and add to the skillet with the onions and mushrooms. Add the chopped dill, if using, and season with salt and pepper.

Cook's Note

An even easier option is to pan-fry the pierogies over medium heat in 2 tablespoons vegetable oil until crisp. Sprinkle with crushed red pepper.

Farfalle with Clams and Radicchio

Clams and tomatoes give up their sweetness to this sauce, while the radicchio adds a bracingly bitter note.

1 heaping teaspoon salt, plus more to taste

1 teaspoon extra-virgin olive oil

1/2 cup diced plum (Roma) tomatoes or diced canned tomatoes

1/2 cup shredded radicchio

1/2 teaspoon finely chopped garlic

1/2 cup canned or homemade chicken broth (page 50) or water

3 ounces farfalle (butterfly-shaped pasta) or other short pasta

1/2 cup drained whole clams (half a 10-ounce can) or shucked fresh clams

1 Combine 6 cups water and 1 heaping teaspoon salt in a medium saucepan. Bring to a boil.

2 Meanwhile, heat the olive oil over medium heat in a skillet large enough to hold the cooked pasta. Cook the tomatoes, radicchio, and garlic until soft, about 10 minutes. Stir in the chicken broth and simmer a few minutes longer.

3 Add the pasta to the boiling water, stirring to separate the pieces. Cook until al dente. Drain.

4 Mix the pasta and clams into the tomato mixture. Taste, and add salt as needed.

Cook's Note

Use leftover clams within a day or two as an addition to vegetable soup, a tomato-based sauce for pasta, or in Linguine Aglio e Olio (page 71).

MAKES 1 SERVING
PREP: 5 MINUTES
COOK: 10 MINUTES

Fettuccine with Smoked Salmon and Peas

Occasionally I crave pasta with a creamy sauce. With its sprightly hint of lemon, this luxurious dish satisfies the yen.

1/2 tablespoon butter

1 tablespoon finely chopped shallot or onion

2 tablespoons heavy cream

Freshly ground black or white pepper

1/3 cup frozen baby peas (thawed) (see Note)

1/2 ounce smoked salmon, cut into thin strips (about 2 tablespoons)

1/4 teaspoon finely chopped lemon zest (see Note)

1 heaping teaspoon salt, plus a pinch

3 ounces dried fettuccine (or 4 ounces fresh)

1 Melt the butter in a small saucepan over medium heat and add the shallot. Cook and stir until tender. Add the cream along with a pinch of salt and a little pepper. Reduce the heat to low and cook for a few minutes until the sauce thickens slightly. Remove from the heat and stir in the peas, salmon, and lemon zest.

2 Meanwhile, combine 6 cups cold water and 1 heaping teaspoon salt in a medium saucepan. Bring to a boil over high heat. Add the fettuccine, stirring to submerge and separate the strands. Cook until al dente, about 5 to 7 minutes, or 3 minutes for fresh pasta. Drain the pasta, reserving a few tablespoons of the cooking liquid, and return it to the saucepan.

3 Stir a little pasta water into the cream mixture if it seems too thick to coat the pasta evenly. Add to the pasta and stir to combine.

Cook's Note

Remove the yellow part of the lemon peel with a zester or vegetable peeler, and chop with a knife.

Penne with Savory Broccoli Sauce

1 heaping teaspoon salt

**1 medium broccoli crown (see Note), cut into small pieces
  (about 2 cups)**

1 cup penne, orecchiette, or cavatelli (about 3 ounces)

1 tablespoon extra-virgin olive oil

1 teaspoon finely chopped garlic

1 anchovy

Crushed red pepper, to taste

Freshly grated Parmigiano-Reggiano cheese

1 Combine 6 cups water and the salt in a medium saucepan. Bring to a boil over high heat. Boil the broccoli for a minute or two until the stalks are barely tender (test with a knife). Scoop out the broccoli with a slotted spoon and set aside. Add the pasta to the same water.

2 Meanwhile, heat the oil over medium-low heat in a medium skillet. Add the garlic and cook until golden, about a minute. Add the anchovy along with 1/3 cup of the pasta cooking water, and stir until the anchovy dissolves. Add the reserved broccoli to the mixture. Cover and simmer until the broccoli is tender and some of the liquid has evaporated.

3 Drain the pasta when it is al dente and stir into the broccoli mixture. Transfer to a shallow soup/pasta bowl and season with crushed red pepper and Parmigiano-Reggiano.

Cook's Notes

—Instead of broccoli, you can substitute the same quantity of broccolini or broccoli rabe.

—If you're tempted to ditch the anchovy, please reconsider. This feisty little fish can be subtle. Rather than slapping you with a fishy, salty taste, as it does on a pizza, the anchovy melts unobtrusively into the sauce and gives it a grounded, savory flavor.

—Look for anchovies in olive oil, imported from Spain or Italy— preferably in a glass jar, which makes it easier to save what's left in the refrigerator.

Variation

Add 2 ounces cooked sweet or hot Italian sausage chunks.

MAKES 1 GENEROUS OR 2 MODERATE SERVINGS
PREP: 15 MINUTES
COOK: 10 MINUTES

Spicy Rice Noodles with Pork

In this deeply satisfying dish, the shredded vegetables and meat slivers disperse evenly among the noodles so that every bite has a little of everything.

2 ounces dried rice noodles (sticks) or cellophane noodles (see Note)

1 tablespoon black bean and garlic sauce (see Note)

2 teaspoons soy sauce

3 ounces boneless thin-cut pork chop (or chicken breast or sirloin steak)

1/2 medium carrot

1/2 celery rib

1 scallion

2 teaspoons peanut or other vegetable oil, divided

2 teaspoons finely chopped or grated ginger root

Crushed red pepper, to taste

1 Place the noodles in a bowl. Cover with boiling water and let stand until they soften, about 10 minutes; drain. Combine the black bean sauce with the soy sauce and 1/3 cup water in a small bowl; set aside.

2 Cut the pork into thin (1/4-inch) strips. Cut several lengthwise slices of carrot with a potato peeler; stack the slices and cut lengthwise into very thin strips about 3 inches long (julienne). Slice the celery and scallion in the same way. Set aside.

3 In a saucepan, bring 1 quart water to a boil. Add the drained noodles and, after the water returns to a boil, cook for about 5 seconds until soft; drain.

4 Meanwhile, heat 1 teaspoon of the oil over medium-high heat in a skillet or-small wok. Stir-fry the ginger for a few seconds, add the pork, and continue to stir-fry until the pork is no longer pink. Transfer the pork to a bowl.

5 Add the remaining 1 teaspoon oil. Stir-fry the carrot, celery, and scallion for a couple of minutes until crisp-tender. Return the pork to the skillet. Stir in the bean-sauce mixture and the hot noodles. Season with crushed red pepper.

Cook's Notes

—For the cellophane noodles, you can substitute the precooked Asian wheat noodles sold in some produce departments. Add the noodles to the stir-fried mixture and cook, stirring, until hot.

—Black bean and garlic sauce is readily available on the Asian shelves of your supermarket. Look for the Lee Kum Kee brand.

—Rather than wielding a knife yourself, use the shredded vegetables available in many produce departments.

MAKES 1 SERVING
PREP: 10 MINUTES, PLUS MARINATING TIME
COOK: 12 MINUTES

Spaghetti with Fresh Tomato, Basil, and Garlic

A thin skin and a sweet smell are clues, but the only sure way to judge a tomato is to bite into one. When the verdict is thumbs up, make this uncooked sauce that tastes like the essence of summer. Once sauced, the pasta tastes good either hot or at room temperature.

1 medium ripe tomato

4–6 fresh basil leaves

1 + 1/2 tablespoons extra-virgin olive oil

1 teaspoon finely chopped garlic

1 heaping teaspoon salt, plus more to taste

Freshly ground black pepper, to taste

3 ounces spaghetti or capellini

1/3 cup diced fresh mozzarella (optional)

1 Using a sharp knife, strip away the skin of the tomato and cut out the stem end. Remove the seeds with your fingers and use your hand to strain them, letting the juices fall into a large bowl. Roughly chop the tomato flesh, and transfer the tomato and any juices on the cutting board to the bowl. (Alternatively, don't bother peeling and seeding the tomato. Just remove the stem end, chop, and add to the bowl.)

2 Tear the basil leaves into small pieces and add to the bowl, along with the olive oil, garlic, salt, and pepper. Let stand at room temperature for at least 15 minutes (do not refrigerate).

3 Combine 6 cups water and 1 heaping teaspoon salt in a medium saucepan. Bring to a boil over high heat. Add the spaghetti, stirring to submerge and separate the strands. Cook until al dente. Drain and mix gently with the tomato sauce and mozzarella (if using).

Variation

Spaghetti with Fresh Tomato and Avocado: In place of the basil leaves and pepper, add 1 tablespoon chopped cilantro leaves. Just before eating, gently stir in 1/4 to 1/2 cup diced Hass avocado.

Asian Noodles with Spicy Peanut Sauce

Getting the balance of flavors right in a peanut sauce isn't easy but my daughter Kate did it. This one tastes great as a dipping sauce for stir-fried tofu as well as a sauce for noodles.

2 tablespoons natural (unhomogenized) peanut butter

1 tablespoon rice vinegar

2 teaspoons soy sauce

1 teaspoon firmly packed brown sugar

1 small clove garlic, pressed

1/4 teaspoon chili oil, or hot sauce

2 ounces Asian wheat noodles, such as somen or linguine

1 Combine the peanut butter, rice vinegar, soy sauce, brown sugar, garlic, and chili oil with 2 teaspoons water in a small jar. Cover and shake until blended.

2 Meanwhile, bring 1 quart water to a boil in a medium saucepan. Add the noodles and cook until soft but not mushy, 2 to 3 minutes (linguine will take close to 10 minutes). Drain and turn the noodles into a shallow soup/pasta bowl. Add the sauce and toss well.

Marinara Magic

Store-bought sauces

You are likely to find a dozen brands of tomato-based pasta sauce in your supermarket. A few may have a long-cooked, unpleasant taste, but most fall into the middle range—acceptable, but bland. Most contain sugar or corn syrup, making them too sweet for my taste.

Prepared marinara sauces are undeniably convenient, though, and with luck you may find one with the aroma and taste of a good homemade sauce. Rao's Homemade is one that I like. If you can't find that, keep tasting until you find a worthy alternative.

You can buy tomato-based sauces containing extra ingredients such as eggplant or mushrooms, but only rarely do the flavors of the additional ingredients come through in a pronounced way. Some ingredients, such as roasted garlic, can give an acrid taste to the sauce. I prefer to buy a plain tomato-based sauce and enhance it at home.

Sauces with something extra

Whether you make your own tomato-based sauce or buy a good ready-made brand, adding an extra ingredient or two can make it taste more interesting.

Survey your pantry or refrigerator for inspiration, or try these combinations, all proportioned for a 3-ounce pasta serving.

● **Tuna:** Brown 1 crushed garlic clove in 1 teaspoon olive oil; remove the garlic clove, stir in 1/2 cup tomato-based sauce and cook until hot. Remove from the heat and stir in 2 pitted, sliced black or green olives, 5 rinsed capers, and 2 to 3 tablespoons drained flaked tuna. Stir into cooked spaghetti or other pasta.

● **Shiitake-onion:** Sauté 1/2 cup thinly sliced shiitake caps with 2 tablespoons finely chopped scallion or shallot in 2 teaspoons olive oil; stir in 1/2 cup tomato-based sauce and cook until hot. Stir into cooked orecchiette or other short pasta.

● **Rapid ragu:** Sauté 2 ounces ground beef, ground turkey, or Italian sausage (casing removed) with 2 tablespoons finely chopped onion or shallot; stir in 1/2 cup tomato-based sauce and simmer 15 minutes; mix in the cooked pasta and top with freshly grated Parmigiano-Reggiano.

● **Pasta e fagioli:** Heat 1/2 cup tomato-based sauce with 3/4 cup drained white beans. Stir into cooked elbow pasta and add 1 tablespoon chopped fresh flat-leaf parsley.

MAKES ABOUT 2 + 1/2 CUPS
PREP: 15 MINUTES
COOK: 1 HOUR

Homemade Tomato Sauce

This versatile tomato-based sauce is nice to have on hand, for pizza as well as pasta. Make sure the tomatoes, the main ingredient, are top quality. I prefer canned tomatoes imported from Italy (if you spot San Marzano on the label, that's good).

1 tablespoon extra-virgin olive oil

1/2 cup chopped onion

1 teaspoon finely chopped or pressed garlic

1–2 anchovies (optional)

1/4 teaspoon dried oregano or Italian seasoning

1 large (28-ounce) can whole tomatoes in juice or puree

1 tablespoon tomato paste (from a tube)

1/2 teaspoon salt

1/4 teaspoon freshly ground black pepper

1 In a large saucepan, heat the oil over medium heat. Sauté the onion until tender and golden, about 5 minutes. Stir in the garlic, anchovy (if using), and oregano. Cook until aromatic, about 1 minute.

2 Drain the tomato juices into the pan, holding back the tomatoes with a spoon or spatula. Crush the tomatoes between your fingers, letting the pulp fall into the pan. Stir in the tomato paste, salt, and pepper.

3 When the mixture begins to bubble gently, reduce the heat to low. Partially cover the saucepan to prevent splattering, and simmer until the sauce is thick, about 1 hour. Cool.

4 Transfer any sauce you will not use within a week to recloseable plastic bags or other containers that hold about 1 cup (2 servings). Seal, label, and freeze.

<u>Variations</u>

—Tomato-Pancetta Sauce: Cut 1 thick (1/4-inch) slice pancetta (unsmoked Italian bacon) into small cubes. Add to the saucepan with the onion and proceed as directed above.

—Tomato-Mushroom Sauce: In step 1, sauté 1 cup sliced or quartered white or cremini mushrooms in the saucepan over medium-high heat in 1 teaspoon olive oil. Remove to a plate while proceeding with the recipe, then return the mushrooms to the saucepan with the tomatoes.

Pesto

Pesto is another great "for the freezer" sauce. For maximum convenience, divide it first into solo-size servings—then, all you need to do is mix in a little cheese and it's pasta-ready. Pesto also makes a good sandwich spread or marinade for a chicken breast.

2 cups fresh basil leaves (torn in half if large)

1/2 cup extra-virgin olive oil

2 tablespoons pine nuts, pecans, or walnuts

2 cloves garlic, lightly crushed

1 teaspoon salt

Freshly grated Parmigiano-Reggiano

1 Combine the basil, olive oil, pine nuts, garlic, and salt in a blender or food processor. Blend at high speed, stopping once or twice to scrape down the sides, until smooth. After reserving the amount you plan to use over the next couple of days, spoon the remaining pesto into ice cube trays; freeze.

2 Transfer the frozen pesto cubes to recloseable plastic bags. For a single serving, thaw 1 cube (equal to 2 tablespoons). Or, you can spoon the pesto into resealable containers, each holding 1/4 cup (2 servings); seal, label, and freeze.

3 When you're ready to use fresh or thawed pesto, blend in about 1 tablespoon cheese per serving.

Variations

—Minty Pesto: Replace up to 1/2 cup of the basil with fresh mint leaves.

—Winter Pesto: In place of the basil, substitute roughly chopped arugula leaves or flat-leaf parsley.

—Pesto Provençal: Per serving, along with cheese, stir in 1/4 cup diced tomatoes and 2 tablespoons of halved, pitted niçoise or other flavorful olives.

meaty dishes

Meat that Makes the Cut

Easy Ways with Chicken

- Spicy Marinated Chicken Breast
- Chicken Saltimbocca
- Roast Baby Hen with Root Vegetables
- Chicken and Baby Bok Choy Stir-Fry
- Chicken and Olive Ragouts

Chops, Fillets, and More

- Steak au Poivre
- Grilled Lamb Chops
- Panfried Pork Scaloppine
- Teriyaki-Glazed Pork Tenderloin

Stews and Such

- Belgian Beef Stew
- Posole Presto

Lots of the main dishes I like, from a cheese omelet to a hearty salad, happen to be meatless. So when meat is on my menu, it's a little special, and I want to make something really good. Hence the recipes in this chapter, which are worthy of any company meal but simple to make just for yourself.

Cutlets and chops are God's gift to the solo cook. Instead of coping with a roast, you can buy a chicken cutlet or steak just the right size for dinner. Pork tenderloin is also a petite cut, perfect for solo cooks. Another blessing: These small, tender cuts taste best when quickly sautéed or grilled, with a few simple seasonings.

Knowing how to roast a small hen or braise meat in a little wine comes in handy, too. Beef stew is a little pokier but worth the wait when you're making enough for more than one meal.

Meat that makes the cut

When I buy meat, I look for the right cut, but I'm also interested in its source. Whenever possible, I buy organic meat from animals that have eaten all-natural feed free of antibiotics and growth-inducing hormones. I also want to know that they have been raised in a humane way, preferably in a small-scale operation—both for the sake of the animals and because those conditions result in meat that is more healthful and likely to taste better. It's getting easier to find and identify high-quality meat.

Sources to try:

● Some supermarkets and specialty stores offer organic choices, and a few chains, such as Whole Foods, sell only "naturally raised" meat.

● Many farmers' markets sell meat from local farms. It's often described as "grass-fed" or "farm-raised"—ask a few questions to find out what is meant by those terms.

● A good mail-order source is nimanranch.com (beef, pork, and lamb). Their website also has information on local retailers in your area.

Spicy Marinated Chicken Breast

This basic method for marinating and cooking chicken breast cutlets can be varied endlessly. In place of the spicy seasoning and oil, for instance, you could rub the chicken with Indian or Thai curry paste.

1/8 teaspoon spicy seasoning blend (jerk, Cajun, tandoori)
2 teaspoons vegetable oil
4–5 ounces chicken breast cutlets or tenders, or a turkey cutlet
1 small lime or lemon wedge

1 Combine the seasoning blend and oil in a 1-quart resealable plastic bag.

2 Slide the chicken into the bag and turn it over several times until evenly coated with the seasoning. Close the bag, pressing out any air. Marinate for 15 minutes at room temperature or refrigerate it for up to 12 hours.

3 Preheat an outdoor grill to medium hot, or heat a nonstick skillet over medium heat. Cook the chicken until both sides are golden brown and the center is no longer pink, 3 to 5 minutes.

4 Squeeze the lime wedge over the chicken.

MAKES 1 SERVING
PREP: 5 MINUTES
COOK: 10 MINUTES

Chicken Saltimbocca

This slightly simplified version of saltimbocca, the famous Roman dish whose name means "jump in the mouth," is made with chicken instead of the traditional veal scaloppine.

1 chicken cutlet (about 5 ounces)

Salt and freshly ground black pepper

4–5 fresh sage leaves

1 thin slice (about 1/2 ounce) prosciutto di Parma

1 teaspoon extra-virgin olive oil

2 tablespoons white wine or dry white vermouth

1 Lay the chicken on a cutting board and, if necessary, pound it lightly to an even thickness (see Note). Sprinkle one side lightly with salt and pepper. Flip the fillet; arrange the sage leaves and then the prosciutto on top, pressing with your palm to make them adhere.

2 Heat the oil in a medium skillet over medium heat. Carefully—so that the prosciutto doesn't fall off—lay the fillet prosciutto-side down in the skillet. When it has browned, after about 1 minute, turn and sear on the other side.

3 Reduce the heat to low and add the wine and about 2 tablespoons water. Partially cover and simmer until the chicken is cooked through, about 5 minutes.

Cook's Note

If you don't have a meat pounder, use the bottom of a small heavy saucepan.

Roast Baby Hen with Root Vegetables

Roast a whole chicken and you'll be sorry—it's just too much of a good thing. But a baby hen is the right size for a solo meal or two. Cooking the small bird with the back facing up keeps the breast from drying out. An assortment of root vegetables, nicely browned, completes the meal.

1 tablespoon extra-virgin olive oil

1/2 teaspoon plus a pinch salt

1/2 teaspoon dried thyme

1/8 teaspoon freshly ground black pepper

1 rock Cornish hen or poussin (baby chicken) (about 1 + 1/4 pounds)

1 clove garlic, crushed

1 small onion, peeled and quartered

1 small russet potato (peeled) or red-skinned potato, cut into chunks

3/4 cup baby carrots

1 Preheat the oven to 425°F. Combine the olive oil with 1/2 teaspoon salt, thyme, and pepper.

2 Rinse the hen and pat dry with a paper towel. Place it breast side down in an ovenproof skillet (preferably cast iron) large enough to hold the hen and vegetables, or a small roasting pan. Pulling the wings and legs to the sides, press down on the back to flatten the hen as much as possible.

3 Rub the skin with crushed garlic and insert what's left in the throat cavity, along with a pinch of salt. Rub half of the olive oil mixture over the hen.

4 Add the onion, potato, and carrots to the bowl with the rest of the olive oil mixture and turn them with your hands until well coated. Arrange the vegetables in a single layer around the chicken.

5 Roast the hen and vegetables in the center of the oven, stirring the vegetables once or twice, until browned and tender, about 40 minutes. Turn the hen and cook for a few minutes until the breast skin browns.

MAKES 1 SERVING
PREP: 10 MINUTES
COOK: 5 MINUTES

Chicken and Baby Bok Choy Stir-Fry

When you're stir-frying for yourself rather than a crowd, you can skip the usual cover-and-simmer stage that comes at the end and, instead, let the sizzling liquid cook the meat while it reduces into a sauce. Spoon the stir-fry over hot rice or Chinese wheat noodles, or let it go solo onto your plate.

4–5 ounces boneless skinless chicken thigh or breast meat, sliced into strips or 1-inch chunks

1/2 teaspoon minced or pressed garlic

1/2 teaspoon grated ginger root

1/4 cup water or chicken broth

1 tablespoon Chinese oyster sauce

2 teaspoons vegetable oil

1 + 1/2 cups chopped baby bok choy or watercress

1 Place the chicken in a small bowl. With your hand or a spatula, mix in the garlic and ginger (at this point, the chicken can be covered and refrigerated for up to 12 hours). In a liquid measuring cup, combine the water with the oyster sauce.

2 Heat the oil in a medium wok or skillet over medium-high heat. Add the chicken and stir-fry until it loses the raw look, about 2 minutes.

3 Add the oyster sauce mixture and continue to stir-fry for a couple of minutes until the chicken is cooked through. Add the bok choy and cook a minute or two until just tender (if using watercress, cook a few seconds until slightly wilted).

Optional Add-Ins

chopped scallion, peanuts, or cashews

MAKES 1 SERVING
PREP: 10 MINUTES
COOK: 12 MINUTES

Chicken and Olive Ragouts

Braising sounds like a process that takes hours—and sometimes it does. But boneless, skinless chicken thighs can be transformed into a robust Ragouts in a matter of minutes. Spoon the saucy chicken over rice or couscous, or enjoy it with crusty bread.

2 teaspoons extra-virgin olive oil

2 boneless skinless chicken thighs, cut into large (1 + 1/2-inch) chunks

1 heaping tablespoon chopped shallot or onion

1–2 plum tomatoes, diced (about 3/4 cup)

1/8 teaspoon salt

Pinch of freshly ground black pepper

2 tablespoons dry white vermouth or wine

4 pitted imported black or green olives, halved or quartered

1 Heat the oil in a medium skillet over medium heat. Cook the chicken, turning the pieces as they brown. Sprinkle the shallot in the spaces around the chicken and cook, stirring, until lightly browned.

2 Add the tomatoes, salt, and pepper. Stir in the vermouth and 1/4 cup water. When the liquid comes to a simmer, reduce the heat to low. Simmer, covered, until the chicken is cooked through and the tomatoes soften to form a thick sauce, 8 to 10 minutes. Stir in the olives.

Cook's Notes

—You could also use skinless bone-in chicken thighs for this recipe. Leave them whole and simmer about 10 minutes longer.

—For a bigger flavor punch, use herb-marinated olives, homemade (page 210) or from a deli, or slice a couple of garlic-stuffed martini olives.

MEATY DISHES

MAKES 1 OR 2 SERVINGS
PREP: 5 MINUTES
COOK: 10 MINUTES

Steak au Poivre

A good steak can stand on its own, without a lot of seasoning. But I make an exception for generous quantities of coarsely ground black pepper, which not only brings out all that beefy flavor but also allows you to give your dinner a fancy French name. Salad always tastes good with a steak, or you might consider smashed potatoes (page 152) or garlicky Swiss chard (page 154).

1 boneless steak (about 8 ounces) (see Notes)
1–2 teaspoons black peppercorns
1/4 teaspoon salt
1 teaspoon grapeseed oil or other vegetable oil
1/4 cup Cabernet or other full-bodied red wine

1 Trim all but a thin border of fat from the steak. Using a mortar and pestle—or, if you don't have one, a potato masher or meat pounder and a sturdy stainless-steel bowl—pound the peppercorns until broken into coarse particles (see Note). Blot the steak dry with a paper towel; sprinkle both sides with salt and the crushed pepper, pressing them into the steak with your palm.

2 Heat the oil in a heavy skillet (preferably cast iron) over medium heat. Sear the steak on one side; turn it and sear on the other. Reduce the heat to low and pour the wine and 1/2 cup water over the steak. Partially cover and cook, spooning the liquid over the steak from time to time, until done the way you like it (about 6 minutes altogether for medium-rare) (see Note).

3 Remove the steak to a plate and let it rest for several minutes. Cook the liquid a little longer, until it reaches a saucy consistency—or, if it is already too thick, add a little wine or water. Drizzle the sauce over the steak.

Cook's Notes

—Choose a fairly thick, well-marbled cut such as a shell steak, porterhouse, rib-eye, or filet mignon.

—Remove the steak from the refrigerator about half an hour before you plan to eat; it will cook more evenly and predictably if it's not chilled.

—Pounding the peppercorns by hand produces a coarser grind than you can get from a pepper mill and delivers a steak with a wonderfully peppery crust. If that's more trouble than you signed on for, just grind some pepper in the usual way.

—Timing a steak is a helpful but, to be honest, not foolproof way to achieve the desired results. As any restaurant grill cook knows, pressing the steak with a thumb provides an extra clue: A rare steak feels soft; one that yields slightly but springs back is medium-rare; if it feels firm, it's well done.

Grilled Lamb Chops

The ideal companions for these chops are Greek salad (page 40) and warm pita.

2 lamb loin chops or 3 rib chops (about 5 ounces total)
1 teaspoon vegetable oil
1 clove garlic, crushed
Salt and freshly ground black pepper
1 small lemon wedge

1 Preheat a grill to medium-hot. Blot the chops on both sides with a paper towel, rub with the oil and garlic, and sprinkle lightly with salt and pepper.

2 Grill the chops until browned on both sides but still pink in the center, 4 to 5 minutes.

3 Squeeze lemon juice over the chops just before eating.

Stovetop Method

Heat 1 tablespoon vegetable oil over high heat in a small, heavy skillet. Blot the chops. Rub with 1 tablespoon oil and garlic, and sprinkle lightly with salt and pepper. Brown the chops on both sides; this will take no longer than 1 minute. Lower the heat to medium and cook 4 minutes longer, for medium-rare (deduct a minute for rare chops; add a minute for medium).

Panfried Pork Scaloppine

In this recipe, small, thin-cut pork chops are beaten even thinner before being coated with bread crumbs and panfried. It's a cross-cultural method with affinities to veal scaloppine, Wiener schnitzel, and (you can see my Texas roots here) chicken-fried steak. For a simple one-dish meal, lay your just-cooked cutlet on a bed of lightly dressed salad greens and surround with fresh tomato wedges.

1–2 thin-cut boneless pork chops (about 4 ounces total)

1 egg

1/4 cup panko (see Note) or dried bread crumbs

1 tablespoon vegetable oil

1 lemon wedge

1 With a meat pounder (or a small heavy saucepan), lightly flatten the chops to a uniform thickness.

2 In one small bowl, beat the egg with a fork. Place the panko in another bowl. Coat the chops on both sides with the egg, letting the excess drip back into the bowl. Press the meat into the bread crumbs until well coated on both sides. Discard any remaining egg or crumbs.

3 In a small skillet (preferably nonstick), heat the oil over medium heat. Fry the chops on each side until golden brown and cooked through, about 5 minutes. Just before eating, squeeze lemon juice over the meat.

Cook's Note

Panko, or Japanese bread crumbs seasoned with salt, makes a wonderfully crisp coating for meat, seafood, or vegetables. You'll find panko in a cellophane package in Asian or other specialty stores. Store it in the freezer, removing only the amount needed for a recipe.

MEATY DISHES

Teriyaki-Glazed Pork Tenderloin

Pork tenderloin is a petite cut that adapts well to solo cooking. Just cut off the part you need and freeze the rest for future meals. When you grill the tenderloin, the sugar in the marinade helps caramelize the outside, forming a delicious glaze.

1 tablespoon teriyaki sauce

1 tablespoon pineapple juice (see Note)

1/4 teaspoon grated ginger root

1/4 teaspoon grated garlic

1/2 pork tenderloin (about 8 ounces) (See Note)

1 Combine the teriyaki sauce, pineapple juice, ginger, and garlic in a 1-quart resealable plastic bag. Slide in the tenderloin and turn it several times until well coated with the marinade; seal the bag. Marinate at room temperature for 15 minutes or refrigerate for up to 12 hours.

2 Preheat a grill to medium-hot. Remove the tenderloin from the bag and wipe dry with a paper towel. Combine the marinade with 2 tablespoons water in a small saucepan and bring to a boil (see Note); remove from heat and dilute with a little more water if it seems too thick.

3 Grill the tenderloin, turning it to sear on all sides. Brush the exposed sides with the marinade, continuing to turn the pork until just cooked through, about 15 minutes total.

4 Let the tenderloin rest a few minutes before slicing.

Cook's Notes

—Pork tenderloins generally range in weight from 1 to 1 + 1/2 pounds. Slice crosswise to create two or three smaller pieces; wrap and freeze whatever you are not grilling right away.

—If you like pineapple, you could substitute a little liquid from a small can of pineapple chunks for the pineapple juice. During the last 5 minutes of cooking, grill a skewerful of pineapple chunks alongside the pork, brushing the fruit with the marinade.

—The marinade must be boiled to prevent any bacteria from the raw meat from being reintroduced during the grilling. To avoid contaminating the brush, do not apply the marinade until the meat is seared.

Belgian Beef Stew

This is one recipe to make in quantity to use in different ways. Like most stews, it will taste better the next day—and it freezes beautifully.

1 pound beef stew meat (preferably chuck)

1/2 teaspoon salt, plus more to taste

1/4 teaspoon freshly ground black pepper, plus more to taste

1 teaspoon plus 2 teaspoons grapeseed oil or other vegetable oil

1/4 cup chopped onion

1 teaspoon minced or pressed garlic

1 tablespoon all-purpose flour

1 cup dark beer or ale

1 tablespoon Dijon mustard

1/4 teaspoon dried thyme

1 bay leaf

1 Blot the meat with paper towels. Trim the fat from the beef and cut into large (about 1 + 1/2-inch) chunks. Sprinkle with 1/2 teaspoon salt and 1/4 teaspoon pepper.

2 In a skillet, heat 1 teaspoon of the oil over medium heat. Cook the onion, stirring, until browned and tender. Add the garlic and cook a few seconds until fragrant. Scrape the mixture onto a plate and clean the skillet.

3 Heat the remaining 2 teaspoons oil in the skillet. Add the beef chunks in a single layer, closely spaced but not touching. Turning the beef with tongs, cook until well browned on all sides.

4 Return the onion mixture to the skillet and sprinkle with the flour, stirring for a few seconds until incorporated.

5 Stir in the beer, mustard, thyme, bay leaf, and enough water (about 1 cup) to nearly cover the meat. After the liquid comes to a boil, reduce the heat to low. Cook at a slow simmer, partially covered, until the beef is tender and the liquid thickens, about 1 hour. Taste, and season with more salt and pepper, if needed.

Cook's Note

Refrigerate the extra servings of stew, or freeze in 1-cup plastic containers.

Single-Serving Suggestions

—Beef Stew, Plain and Simple: Reheat a serving of stew in the microwave or in a saucepan over low heat (add a little water if it seems too thick). Eat it with a green vegetable or over egg noodles, rice, or polenta.

—Beef Stew with Root Vegetables: Steam or microwave 1/2 cup diced potato and 1/2 cup halved baby carrots. Drain, add 1 serving of stew and cook until the beef is heated through. Season to taste with salt and pepper.

—Beef Stew with Mushrooms: In a medium skillet, sauté 1 cup quartered mushrooms (such as cremini or shiitake caps) in 1 teaspoon butter or oil. Reduce heat to low, add 1 serving stew and cook a few minutes until heated through.

Posole Presto

This recipe for posole, the Mexican marriage of pork and hominy, omits the pigs' feet and cuts a few other culinary corners to produce a savory stew in less than an hour. You can eat some right away, but the posole will have a richer, more stewlike character after being reheated the next day.

1 dried chile (such as ancho or New Mexico red) (see Note)

1 + 1/2 cups canned hominy (from a 15-ounce can), drained and rinsed

1 boneless pork chop (4–5 ounces), trimmed and cut into 1/2-inch cubes

1/3 cup chopped onion

1/2 teaspoon salt

1 small zucchini, cut into 1/2-inch cubes

1 Bring about 1 quart water to a boil in a kettle or saucepan. Break the chile into several pieces, discarding the stem, veins, and seeds. Place the chile pieces in a small bowl and cover with some of the boiling water. Allow to stand until soft, about 10 minutes; drain.

2 Place the chile pieces in a blender or food processor with half of the hominy and 1 cup of the hot water; puree until thick but somewhat chunky.

3 Combine the pork cubes, onion, and salt in a medium saucepan. Stir in the hominy-chile blend. Bring to a simmer, cover, and cook gently until the pork is tender, about 15 minutes.

4 Add the zucchini and remaining hominy to the stew, and pour in enough hot water to barely cover the ingredients. Cook, partially covered, over low heat until the zucchini is tender and the flavors are blended.

Cook's Note

In some parts of the country, notably the Southwest, dried chiles are readily available in supermarkets. Otherwise, look for them in specialty stores or online.

simply seafood

Seafood Selection Tips

Savory Ideas for Fish

- Steamed Flounder with Tomatoes and Peppers
- Roasted Halibut with Sweet Miso Sauce
- Grilled Tuna with Mango Dipping Sauce
- Salmon Packet with Sicilian Flavors
- My Mom's Salmon Croquettes

Shellfish Sampler

- Shellfish Steamer
- Sizzling Shrimp with Garlic
- Boiled Shrimp, Hot and Cold
- Panko-Crusted Soft-Shell Crabs

There are exceptions but, for the most part, fish and shellfish are not a "for later" purchase. Buy it fresh to cook that evening. If you know you'll be eating at home two days in a row, consider preparing an extra serving to enjoy chilled the next day, perhaps in a salad.

For a serves-one cook, seafood is great because it doesn't call for a lot of fussing. Brief cooking and a gentle hand with seasonings are usually best. Fish fillets and most kinds of shellfish take extremely well to sautéing, stir-frying, and steaming. If you've chosen a firm-fleshed fish fillet or steak such as salmon, tuna, or cod, the range of options expands to include grilling and roasting.

As a food category, seafood is unusually controversial. With its low calorie count and abundance of omega-3 fatty acids, fish is good for the waistline and cholesterol levels, but didn't I hear a scary story about canned tuna? And what are those endangered species I'm supposed to avoid buying? We all need to be attuned to such issues, of course, but that doesn't mean staying away from seafood altogether. Make the most informed choice you can, and then go home and enjoy your meal.

Seafood selection tips

If possible, buy fish and other seafood from a fish market or counter with knowledgeable personnel. A well-frequented place with brisk turnover of product is best. Raw and cooked seafood should be displayed, separately from each other, in well-chilled cases.

● Find out the sources of the seafood, and get recommendations on the best picks of the day.

● Choose fish fillets with a firm, moist look—never dry or mushy-looking. The skin should have a glistening (not dull) appearance, and the flesh should have a consistent color (not two-tone).

● Seafood should smell faintly of the sea but not have a strong fishy smell. Ask the fishmonger to let you take a sniff of your selection before buying, or hold the packaged seafood close to your nose and take a whiff.

● Check out the frozen food aisle for easy-meal options such as prepared crab cakes, deveined frozen shrimp, and individually wrapped fish fillets.

● Be flexible. You had salmon in mind but the halibut looks fresher? Better to change your plans than be disappointed by the quality of the seafood.

● Visit seafoodchoices.com for advice on sustainable seafood. If you're interested in ordering high-quality seafood by mail, check out wildedibles.com.

Steamed Flounder with Tomatoes and Peppers

This savory stovetop fish dinner is a specialty of Joan Surnamer, a retired New Yorker who has acquired the pleasant habit of buying ingredients for her single-serving dinners at the Union Square greenmarket. Be sure to eat this dish with crusty bread to catch the delicious juices.

2 teaspoons extra-virgin olive oil

1/4 cup chopped onion or shallot

2/3 cup diced fresh tomato

1 small Italian frying pepper, seeded and diced (about 1/2 cup)

2–3 imported black olives, such as Kalamata or niçoise, pitted and slivered (see Note)

1 tablespoon chopped flat-leaf parsley (optional)

5 ounces flounder, turbot, or tilapia fillets, or other mild-flavored fish

Salt and freshly ground black pepper

1 Heat the oil in a small skillet (preferably nonstick) over low heat. Cook the onion, covered, until translucent, about 3 minutes. Add the tomato and Italian pepper; cover, and simmer until the tomato softens, about 10 minutes. The tomato juices may provide enough moisture, but if the mixture seems dry, add a little water.

2 Stir in the olives and, if using, the parsley. Arrange the flounder on top of the vegetables, and season with salt and pepper. Cover and simmer until the fish is milky white and just cooked through, about 5 minutes.

Cook's Note

Place the olives on a cutting board and gently press down with the flat of a cook's knife. The pits will separate from the flesh, allowing easy removal.

Roasted Halibut with Sweet Miso Sauce

Mild-mannered fish gets an instant injection of flavor through the alchemy of a deep-brown sauce made with just three ingredients.

2 teaspoons mirin (Japanese sweet rice wine)

1 teaspoon dark miso (fermented soybean paste)

1 teaspoon sugar

5–6 ounces halibut (cod or another firm, white-fleshed fish can be substituted)

1 Preheat the oven to 450°F. Combine the mirin, miso, and sugar in a small microwave-safe dish; microwave just until the mixture liquifies, about 20 seconds (alternatively, heat in a small saucepan on the stove).

2 Place the fillet in an ovenproof skillet or dish and spoon the miso sauce over it. Roast until the fish is just cooked through, about 8 minutes.

MAKES 1 TO 2 SERVINGS
PREP: 10 MINUTES
COOK: 6 MINUTES

Grilled Tuna with Mango Dipping Sauce

This is a stylish dish that you might be tempted to order in a restaurant, but why bother when it's so easy to make at home? If there are leftovers, both the tuna and the mango sauce taste delicious chilled. Couscous and sautéed snow peas would make great go-alongs.

1 teaspoon grapeseed oil or other vegetable oil

1 teaspoon soy sauce

8-ounce tuna steak (about 1-inch thick) (see Note)

1 cup loosely packed fresh mango cubes (see Note)

2 teaspoons lime juice

2 teaspoons cilantro leaves

1/8 teaspoon salt

1/8–1/4 teaspoon jarred Asian chili paste (sambal oelek), or hot pepper sauce, to taste

1 Preheat a grill to medium-hot. Rub the oil and then the soy sauce over both sides of the tuna steak. Let the tuna stand while you prepare the mango sauce.

2 In a blender, combine the mango, lime juice, cilantro, salt, and chili paste (starting with 1/8 teaspoon and adjusting for taste) with 2 tablespoons water. Pulse until smooth, adding a little more water if the sauce seems too thick. Pour the sauce into a small bowl for dipping.

3 Grill the tuna steak, turning once, to desired doneness, about 6 minutes total for medium-rare. Place the steak and dipping sauce on a dinner plate; dip each bite of tuna in the sauce.

Cook's Notes

—Tuna steaks usually weigh about 1 pound each, but my fishmonger is perfectly willing to cut one in half, and I'll bet yours will, too. If not, tuna freezes extremely well, so you could just stockpile the other serving for a future meal.

—How to cut a mango: Holding the mango on a board with the narrower end facing up, slice along each side of the pit to cut off the "cheeks." Score the flesh criss-cross, taking care not to cut through the skin. With a knife or large spoon, remove the cubes. Peel the center section and cut off the remaining fruit. Enjoy any extra mango cubes alone or with vanilla yogurt or ice cream.

MAKES 1 SERVING
PREP: 5 MINUTES
COOK: 12 MINUTES

Salmon Packet with Sicilian Flavors

I first encountered this dish in a cooking class taught by Mark Strausman, a New York chef, and have since made it dozens of times. The foil packet seals in the vibrant Southern Italian flavors.

5-ounce salmon fillet

Salt and freshly ground black pepper

1/2 teaspoon extra-virgin olive oil

2–3 thin lemon slices

3 oil-cured Sicilian olives or other small, flavorful olives

1/2 teaspoon small capers, rinsed

1 Preheat the oven to 500°F (see Note). Tear off a 12-inch square piece of aluminum foil and place it shiny side down on the countertop (see Note). Lay the salmon fillet in the center. Season to taste with salt and pepper, drizzle with olive oil, and arrange the lemon slices on top. Scatter the olives and capers around the salmon.

2 Draw together the long edges of foil and fold over several times, crimping tightly to prevent leakage but leaving room inside the packet for heat circulation; fold each remaining edge to seal in the same way.

3 Place the packet on a baking sheet. Cook for 12 minutes. Transfer the packet to a dinner plate and let it rest for a couple of minutes before opening.

Cook's Notes

—The packet can also be cooked successfully in a toaster oven but will probably need a little more cooking time, about 15 minutes altogether.

—This dinner can also be enclosed in a square of parchment paper.

My Mom's Salmon Croquettes

I grew up on the Gulf Coast, but, with the exception of shrimp, fresh fish and shellfish rarely showed up on our family dinner table. Canned-salmon croquettes did, however, and I still think they're quite tasty. It's the kind of meal you can make on the spur of the moment from ingredients on hand in your kitchen. I like to eat it with a big mess of spinach, sautéed with olive oil and garlic, and splashed with white wine vinegar.

1 can (6 ounces) pink salmon, drained (3/4 cup)

1/4 cup cracker crumbs (see Note)

1 egg white

2 tablespoons finely chopped shallot or onion

1/2 teaspoon Dijon mustard, plus more for serving

Olive oil or vegetable oil, for frying

1 Rub the chunks of salmon between your fingers, letting the flakes fall into a small bowl. Add the cracker crumbs, egg white, shallot, and mustard. Stir with a fork until well mixed.

2 Form salmon mixture into 2 patties. If you do not plan to eat both, wrap one in plastic wrap and refrigerate to cook the following day, or freeze.

3 In a small skillet over medium heat, heat 1 teaspoon oil per patty. Cook the salmon until browned on both sides and heated through, about 7 minutes total. Spoon a little more mustard on top, if you like.

Cook's Note

I usually use Stoned Wheat Thins because that's what I have on hand. Saltines work fine, too. My mom made cracker crumbs by placing the crackers between two sheets of waxed paper and crushing them with a rolling pin. You can also pound them with a potato masher (put them in a plastic or metal bowl first) or crush them in a food processor.

MAKES 1 SERVING
PREP: 15 MINUTES
COOK: 5 MINUTES

Shellfish Steamer

This recipe came from a Maine chef by the name of Pamela White, whose whereabouts I no longer know. She developed this quick but delectable method for steaming shellfish by the bushel at a resort during Maine's brief high season; you can do the same thing at home. French bread and a tossed green salad are all that's needed to round out the meal.

10 farm-raised mussels

4 cherrystone (littleneck) clams

1 tablespoon finely chopped shallot or onion

1 teaspoon finely chopped garlic

1 teaspoon butter, cut into bits

1 tablespoon chopped fresh flat-leaf parsley, chervil, tarragon, or thyme

1/2 cup white vermouth or white wine

1 Cover the mussels and clams with cold water; let stand for 10 minutes while you prepare the other ingredients. Remove the shellfish one at a time and scrub under cold running water to remove any grit; with a paring knife, pull off any "beards" clinging to the shells.

2 Place the mussels and clams in a saucepan or deep skillet large enough to hold them in a single layer. Scatter the shallot, garlic, butter, and parsley over the shellfish, and pour the vermouth over them. Cover the pan and place over medium-high heat. Steam the shellfish until they open, about 5 minutes (the mussels will open first); discard any that fail to open. Using tongs, transfer the shellfish to a bowl. Pour the broth over them, straining out the solid ingredients, if you like.

MAKES 1 SERVING
PREP: 10 MINUTES
COOK: 5 MINUTES

Sizzling Shrimp with Garlic

A young, well-travelled relative of ours, Margaret Lydecker, fell in love with this classic Spanish tapa, known as gambas al ajilla, while living in Spain. Her technique calls for letting the oil, garlic, and water "get to know one another" before adding the shrimp.

2 pinches salt (preferably sea salt)
2 tablespoons olive oil
1 garlic clove, sliced
4 ounces jumbo or large shrimp, peeled
Crusty bread

1 Combine the salt and 2 tablespoons water in a small dish.

2 Combine the olive oil and garlic in a small sauté pan, and heat over medium-high heat just until the garlic begins to sizzle and turn golden; don't let it burn. Holding the lid in one hand, add the salted water with the other, and immediately clap the lid on to minimize splattering.

3 After letting the liquid sizzle for 20 seconds or so, lift the lid, add the shrimp, and quickly cover again. Cook just until the shrimp turns pink and the liquid reduces, about 30 seconds, lifting the lid once more to stir.

4 Take the sauté pan directly to the table. Use chunks of bread to scoop up the shrimp and juices. Or, with a fork, spear each bread chunk with a shrimp and dunk in the pan juices. Repeat until the shrimp are gone and the pan is wiped clean.

Cook's Note

This dish cooks in a breathtakingly brief span of time, so it's essential to read the recipe all the way through and have your ingredients at the ready before you begin.

MAKES 2 SERVINGS
PREP: 10 MINUTES
COOK: 3 MINUTES

Boiled Shrimp, Hot and Cold

Here are two more seafood dinners you can eat with your hands. The first night, eat the peel-as-you-go shrimp hot with a lemon-butter dipping sauce and crusty bread. Then start looking forward to tomorrow's treat: chilled shrimp with spicy cocktail sauce.

1 tablespoon plus 1 teaspoon lemon juice

1 teaspoon seafood seasoning (such as Old Bay)

1/2 teaspoon salt

8 ounces unshelled large or jumbo shrimp, rinsed

2 teaspoons butter

1 Combine 1 tablespoon lemon juice, the seafood seasoning, and salt with 1/4 cup water in a medium saucepan. Bring to a boil. Reduce the heat, add the shrimp, and cover the pan. Simmer, turning the shrimp once, just until they turn pink, about 3 minutes. Remove the shrimp to a plate.

2 Meanwhile, melt the butter in a small microwave-safe bowl. Stir in the remaining 1 teaspoon lemon juice and 1 tablespoon of the shrimp cooking liquid.

3 Eat half of the shrimp, dipping them in the lemon-butter sauce. Chill the rest to eat with cocktail sauce the next day.

Cook's Note

You can eat the second day's chilled shrimp with a store-bought cocktail sauce. Or, to make your own sauce, combine 1 tablespoon ketchup with 1 teaspoon lemon juice and a little hot sauce or prepared horseradish. If, like me, you keep jalapeño ketchup on hand, all you need to add is the lemon juice.

MAKES 1 SERVING
PREP: 5 MINUTES
COOK: 3 MINUTES

Panko-Crusted Soft-Shell Crabs

The soft-shell crab season is short (peak season is from June to September), so when they come your way, it's good to be prepared with a tasty recipe. Steamed sugar snap peas or green beans dressed with a little butter and lemon juice would go well with these.

2 soft-shell crabs (about 5 ounces total)

1/4 cup milk

1 egg

Red pepper sauce, such as Tabasco

1/4 cup panko or other dried bread crumbs (see Note)

1 teaspoon grapeseed oil or other vegetable oil

1 teaspoon butter

1 small lemon wedge

1 In a shallow bowl, soak the crabs in the milk for 5 minutes. Meanwhile, beat the egg in another bowl and season liberally with red pepper sauce (keeping in mind that only part of the egg will be used); place the panko in a third bowl. Dip each crab in the egg and coat well with the bread crumbs.

2 Heat the oil and butter in a medium skillet over medium heat until sizzling. Fry the crabs on both sides until well browned, about 3 minutes. Spritz them with lemon juice.

Cook's Note

I find that the seasoning in panko—crisp Japanese bread crumbs sold in Asian food stores—precludes the need for additional salt. Before dipping the crabs, taste your bread crumbs, and add salt if you consider them underseasoned.

beans grains & soy

Beans and Grains: The Basics

Bean Cuisine

- Vegetarian Chipotle Chili
- Chickpea and Spinach Sauté
- One-Pot Bean and Corn Dinner
- Fettunta with White Beans and Greens

Main Grains

- Soft Polenta with Porcini and Gorgonzola
- Risotto with Shiitake Mushrooms and Peas
- Indian-Spiced Fried Rice

Soy and So On

- Golden Fried Tofu

Five-Minute Soy Entrées

Beans, grains, and soy. Hmmm—sounds like bland health food. But once you've tried a few of these dishes, I hope you'll agree that they are far from boring or flavorless. It's easy to find inspiration for preparing these ingredients. Because beans and grains are menu mainstays throughout the world, every country and ethnic group has ideas for bringing out their best.

These recipes are grouped together because all can serve as vegetarian main dishes (when meat is included, it is as an optional ingredient). But if you enjoy a certain recipe, say, the chickpea and spinach sauté, check the index under chickpeas, and it will take you to other chickpea recipes, including hummus and a chickpea-tuna salad.

Beans and grains: the basics

About beans

● Drain canned beans and rinse them to remove salt and other additives.

● Keep in mind that a sixteen-ounce can, drained, contains about two cups of beans—two to three servings.

● If you eat a lot of beans, make them from scratch at least some of the time. Cook flavor into dried beans by simmering them with aromatic ingredients such as celery, carrot, garlic, peppercorns, and fresh herbs (especially parsley stems and leaves). Add salt once the cooking is complete.

● Store cooked beans in the refrigerator for up to five days. To freeze beans, toss them first with a little oil to separate them; pureed beans can also be frozen.

About grains

● Buy rice and other grains in small quantities and seal tightly once the packages are opened. To extend their shelf life, store them in your refrigerator or freezer.

● Experiment with different kinds of rice. For instance, basmati, jasmine, Texmati, and Konriko Wild Pecan rice are interesting long-grain varieties to try.

● For risotto, an imported Italian rice such as Arborio or Carnaroli is best, but Spanish medium-grain rice also works well.

Pilaf method

This easy method works for rice and for other nutrient-rich grains such as bulgur, barley, kasha, and quinoa (rinse quinoa well before using).

In a saucepan set over medium heat, dry-toast the grain, or sauté with chopped onion in butter or oil.

Add the amount of water recommended on the package, along with salt and freshly ground black pepper and, if you wish, an herb. Bring to a boil, reduce the heat, cover, and cook until the liquid is absorbed.

Add butter, if desired, and let the cooked grain stand, off heat, in a covered saucepan, for several minutes. Stir in the butter just before eating.

Vegetarian Chipotle Chili

When life gets too complicated, make this chili. It's always a comfort to come home to a good nourishing meal, and you won't have to worry about cooking for a few days.

2 teaspoons olive oil or other vegetable oil

1/2 cup chopped onion

1/2 cup chopped green or yellow bell pepper

1 teaspoon chopped garlic

1/2 teaspoon ground cumin

2 tablespoons ketchup

1 teaspoon salt, plus more to taste

1/4 teaspoon chipotle hot sauce, or to taste (see Note)

Bean cooking liquid and/or water

2 cups cooked pinto or other red beans

1/2 cup fresh or frozen corn kernels

1 Heat the oil in a medium saucepan over medium heat. Add the onion and bell pepper. Cook, stirring often, until tender, about 5 minutes. Stir in the garlic and cumin, and cook until fragrant, about 1 minute. Add the ketchup, salt, chipotle hot sauce, and 1/4 cup bean liquid or water. Cook and stir several minutes until thick.

2 Add the beans, corn, and enough liquid to cover. Bring to a boil. Reduce the heat to medium-low and simmer, partly covered, about 10 minutes. Taste and add more salt and chipotle sauce, if you like.

Cook's Note

Chipotles are smoked, dried jalapeños with a seductive flavor that makes them wonderful for spicing up whatever you like. The easiest way to incorporate this taste is by adding a splash of chipotle hot sauce. Alternatively, you can use canned chipotles and the adobo sauce in which they are packed. Blend the contents of the can, using a food processor or blender; in a covered container, it can be stored indefinitely in the refrigerator.

Other Add-Ins

tofu cubes, chopped cilantro

Variation

Beef Chipotle Chili: Omit the oil. Combine the onion and bell pepper with 1/2 pound ground beef. Cook the mixture, breaking apart the beef with a wooden spoon, until the beef is no longer pink. Proceed as directed above.

MAKES 1 SERVING
PREP: 10 MINUTES
COOK: 10 MINUTES

Chickpea and Spinach Sauté

With or without rice, this colorful sauté makes a well-balanced meal.

1 tablespoon pine nuts

2 teaspoons extra-virgin olive oil

1/4 cup finely chopped onion or shallot

1/2 teaspoon finely chopped garlic

3 cups baby spinach

1/2 cup canned chickpeas, drained and rinsed

Salt and freshly ground black pepper, to taste

1 In a medium skillet over low heat, toast the pine nuts until lightly browned, stirring often to make sure they do not burn; remove from heat and set aside.

2 Raise the heat to medium and heat the olive oil in the same skillet. Sauté the onion and garlic until tender, about 5 minutes.

3 Add the spinach, chickpeas, and 2 tablespoons water. Season to taste with salt and pepper. Cook, covered, until the spinach wilts and the chickpeas are warm, about 5 minutes. Scatter the toasted pine nuts on top.

One-Pot Bean and Corn Dinner

Living off campus during her last year of college, my daughter Mary had little time to cook and, as a vegetarian, wanted to make sure she was getting the right nutrients. Her solution: this appealing one-pot meal, which requires no chopping or careful measuring, and very little washing up. Mary recommends piling any leftovers on toasted bagel halves or English muffins, or using them as a burrito filling.

1/4 cup white rice

Pinch of salt

2/3 cup frozen corn

1/2 cup frozen leaf spinach from a bag

1 cup canned black beans, drained and rinsed

2 tablespoons hot salsa, or to taste

2 tablespoons grated sharp cheddar cheese, or to taste

1 In a medium saucepan, bring 1/2 cup water to a boil. Add the rice and a pinch of salt. When the water returns to a boil, turn the heat to medium-low and cover the pan. Simmer until the rice swells but is not completely cooked, about 10 minutes.

2 Stir in the corn and spinach. Cook until hot, stirring from time to time to keep the mixture from sticking to the pan. Add the beans and cook a few minutes longer. Serve with salsa and cheddar cheese on top.

Cook's Note

Even quicker: You can substitute instant brown rice for the white rice, cooking it just 2 to 3 minutes before adding the other ingredients.

Optional Add-Ins

chopped sweet onion, scrambled egg

BEANS GRAINS & SOY

MAKES 1 SERVING
PREP: 5 MINUTES
COOK: 8 MINUTES

Fettunta with White Beans and Greens

In this recipe, a savory blend of white beans and greens tops the crisp, garlic-rubbed bread that is known as bruschetta everywhere in Italy except Tuscany, where it is called fettunta. A drizzle of good olive oil provides the finishing touch.

3/4 cup canned or homemade white beans (see Note)

3/4 cup roughly chopped Swiss chard or spinach leaves

2–3 tablespoons chicken broth, bean cooking liquid, or water

Salt and freshly ground black pepper, to taste

1 slice crusty white bread

1 clove garlic, crushed

Extra-virgin olive oil (see Note)

1 Combine the beans, chard, and broth in a small saucepan. Season to taste with salt and pepper. Cover and cook over medium-low heat until the greens wilt, stirring occasionally.

2 Set the toaster oven or toaster on the "light" setting, and toast bread until crisp but not browned. Rub both sides of the warm toast with garlic.

3 Lay the toast on a dinner plate and spoon the beans and greens mixture on top. Drizzle with olive oil and, if you like, grind more pepper on top.

Cook's Notes

—Drain and rinse canned beans before using. Or, to prepare homemade beans: Cook 1 cup dried white beans according to package directions with 1 slice onion, 1 sprig fresh sage, and, if desired, 1 slice pancetta (unsmoked Italian bacon). Save leftover cooked beans for another use.

—If you have a peppery Tuscan olive oil (Coltibuono is a well-distributed brand) or another artisanal olive oil, this is a good time to bring it out.

Soft Polenta with Porcini and Gorgonzola

This is comfort food, Italian style. And, thanks to instant polenta, it is very doable on a small scale. Indulge in a bowlful, followed by a salad. Alternatively, this luxurious polenta pairs well with steak or any roast meat.

4–5 dried porcini slices (about 1/8 ounce)

1 teaspoon butter

2 teaspoons finely chopped shallot or onion

1/4 teaspoon salt

1/4 cup instant polenta

2 tablespoons Gorgonzola cheese, at room temperature

1 Place the porcini in a small bowl and barely cover with boiling water. Let stand until soft, about 10 minutes. Lift out the porcini with a slotted spoon; roughly chop them. Line a small strainer with a paper towel, and strain the porcini liquid into a liquid measuring cup. Fill with water to the 1-cup mark.

2 In a small saucepan over medium heat, melt the butter. Sauté the porcini and shallot until tender, a minute or 2. Add the porcini liquid and salt, and bring to a boil.

3 While stirring with a wooden spoon or heatproof spatula, add the polenta little by little. Adjust the heat so the polenta bubbles gently. Continue stirring until the polenta is very thick, about 5 minutes. If lumps form, whisk with a wire whisk to smooth them out.

4 Remove the saucepan from the heat, add the Gorgonzola, and stir until completely blended with the polenta.

Cook's Note

Any polenta you plan to eat later can be spooned into a heatproof buttered ramekin. Reheat, covered, in a microwave, toaster oven, or oven.

Risotto with Shiitake Mushrooms and Peas

The risotto I make for myself seems to come out a little better than the same recipe made for several people. Indeed, it is worth noting that the best Italian restaurants cook risotto to order, one or two portions at a time. Risotto has the reputation of being laborious, but it's not, particularly. You do need to stir it often, but not constantly. Take the opportunity, while keeping an eye on the simmering rice, to turn on some music and pour yourself a glass of wine.

1 + 1/2 cups store-bought or homemade chicken or vegetable broth (see pages 50 and 48, respectively) (see Note)

1 teaspoon extra-virgin olive oil

2 teaspoons butter, divided

1 tablespoon finely chopped shallot or onion

3/4 cup thinly sliced shiitake caps, cremini, or white mushrooms, or a mixture

1/8 teaspoon dried thyme or leaves from 1 sprig fresh thyme

Salt and freshly ground black pepper, to taste

1/3 cup Arborio, Carnaroli, or other medium-grain Italian rice

2 tablespoons dry white vermouth

1/4 cup frozen or fresh peas

1–2 tablespoons grated Parmigiano-Reggiano cheese

1 Bring the broth to a simmer in a small saucepan over low heat.

2 Heat the olive oil and 1 teaspoon of the butter in a small sauté pan or saucepan (about 6 inches in diameter) over medium heat. Sauté the shallot until tender but not browned. Add the mushrooms and cook, stirring often, until they soften. Add the thyme and season to taste with salt and pepper.

3 Add the remaining 1 teaspoon butter and stir in the rice. Cook and stir for a minute or 2 until the grains are well coated. Add the vermouth and, when most of the liquid has evaporated, ladle in enough warm broth to barely cover the rice. Adjust the heat so the liquid simmers briskly (see Note). Once that is absorbed, replenish with the same amount of broth. Continue to stir often, adding broth as needed, until the rice is cooked but still slightly firm in the center.

4 Remove the pan from the heat and stir in the peas along with a little more broth for the risotto to "drink" while resting for about 5 minutes (don't worry if some broth is left over). Sprinkle with the Parmigiano-Reggiano cheese.

Cook's Notes

—Taste the broth. If you're using prepared broth, you may need to substitute water for part of the broth so that it does not become too salty as it reduces. If the broth is homemade, you may need to add salt.

—The correct heat level is very important to success in making risotto. If the burner is too hot, the rice will cook unevenly; if it's too low it may turn gummy. I use a medium setting throughout the cooking, which is hot enough to sauté the vegetables and to keep the risotto at a brisk simmer once the liquids are added.

MAKES 1 SERVING
PREP: 10 MINUTES
COOK: 20 MINUTES

Indian-Spiced Fried Rice

My husband, Kent, makes this aromatic fried rice as a lunch or a late-evening repast for himself or anyone else who is hungry. He usually makes the rice from scratch, but if you have leftover rice from Indian or Chinese takeout, this is a great way to use it up.

2 teaspoons grapeseed oil or other vegetable oil

1/4 cup chopped onion

1/4 teaspoon garam masala, or to taste (see Note)

1/8 teaspoon salt

1 cup cooked basmati rice (see Note) or other long-grain rice, hot or cold

1/4 cup diced cucumber

1/4 cup diced tomato

1 Heat the oil in a medium skillet over medium heat. Sauté the onion, stirring often, until lightly browned. Stir in the garam masala and salt, and cook until fragrant, a few seconds.

2 Stir in the rice, and spread it in a thin layer over the bottom of the skillet. When the rice starts to brown, stir it and spread it out again, repeating until fried to your liking. If the rice seems to be cooking too quickly, reduce the heat or add a little water. Serve the rice with cucumber and tomato on top.

Cook's Notes

—Garam masala is a blend of up to a dozen roasted, ground spices, including coriander, cumin, cinnamon, black pepper, and chiles.

—Basmati, a delicate, long-grain rice, is found in Indian and Middle Eastern grocery stores and, these days, many supermarkets. I usually rinse imported basmati, checking for impurities, but I skip this step when using U.S.–grown basmati.

—An easy cooking method: Stir 1/3 cup basmati rice into 1 cup boiling water and cook uncovered at a brisk simmer. Start tasting after 8 minutes; as soon as the grains are tender, drain the rice.

Golden Fried Tofu

This tofu is tasty enough to eat on its own, perhaps with rice or a green vegetable, or you could add it to any improvised stir-fry.

1 thick slice extra-firm tofu (about 3 ounces)

1 teaspoon peanut oil or other vegetable oil

2 teaspoons brown sugar

1 teaspoon soy sauce

1 Blot the tofu on both sides with a paper towel and cut into 1-inch cubes. Combine the sugar and soy sauce in a small dish.

2 Heat the oil in a small skillet over medium-high heat. Fry the tofu, turning the pieces until golden brown on several sides.

3 Remove the skillet from the heat and immediately pour the sugar-soy mixture over the tofu. Stir the now-sizzling tofu until it is well coated and turns a darker caramel color.

Five-minute soy entrées

Tofu is not only an excellent protein source, but also seems to be compatible with just about any seasoning or combination of ingredients. Tempeh is made of fermented soybeans, sometimes in combination with grains. It has a firm, meatlike texture and tastes better than it sounds; some patties, such as those made by Lightlife, are flavored with tamari or another marinade.

Without much fanfare, tofu, tempeh, and other soy products can be turned into quick vegetarian entrées such as these:

Seasoned tofu cake

Cut a thick slab (about 3 ounces) of tofu (preferably soft or silken) and lay the "cake" on a plate. Drizzle 1/2 teaspoon sesame oil and 1/2 teaspoon soy sauce over the cake. Sprinkle 1 teaspoon toasted sesame seeds and up to 1 tablespoon chopped scallion on top. Enjoy the tofu cake alone or with rice.

Veggie cheeseburger

Follow package directions for heating a frozen veggie burger or tempeh patty. Lay a thin slice of cheddar or other cheese on top and heat just until it melts. Eat on a sandwich roll spread with honey mustard, mayo, or hummus, and topped with sliced tomato, sweet onion, and lettuce.

Cook's notes

Buy tofu in sealed containers and open only when ready to use. Nasayo, a widely available brand, offers organic tofu in several degrees of firmness. Silken and soft are ideal for soups; firm and extra-firm are the right choices for stir-fries.

Store leftover tofu in water, changing it daily, and use within a week. Tofu can also be frozen; thawed, the texture will be somewhat chewier.

To store tempeh, follow instructions on the package. Tempeh patties in vacuum packaging have a fairly long shelf life when refrigerated or frozen.

strictly vegetables

Cooking Vegetables: The Basics

Easy Ways to Get Your Veggies

Meatless Main Dishes

- Roasted Ratatouille
- Succulent Succotash
- Grilled Chile Relleno
- Pan-Seared Portabellas

Vegetables on the Side

- Southern-Fried Okra
- Creamy Smashed Potatoes
- Spicy Corn on the Cob
- Swiss Chard, Good and Garlicky
- Steamed Asparagus
- Broccoli with Hazelnuts

Sometimes an all-veggie main dish is just what you want. Other times, you need something green to go with a chicken cutlet or pork chop. Whatever their role, vegetables deserve to be selected with care and cooked carefully. It sounds like an oxymoron, but vegetables can and should be exciting. I didn't settle on these recipes just because vegetables are good for you, but rather because these dishes are among my favorite things to eat—and I hope you'll feel that way, too.

If possible, shop in a supermarket that sells most vegetables loose, allowing you to select the amount you need (better yet, find a good produce store or farmer's market). Nature has packaged many vegetables in sizes convenient for single-portion cooking: artichokes, carrots, green beans, and summer squash, to name a few. Baby bok choy and Japanese or Italian eggplants are downsized varieties worth seeking out. Broccoli florets or crowns, sold loose, are just right for a single serving.

When you shop at a farmers' market, you'll know what's in season locally. Otherwise, read labels and signs noting the origin of fresh vegetables, keeping in mind that the closer to your home the produce was grown, the fresher it is likely to be.

Don't rule out frozen vegetables. Peas that were processed soon after harvest may have more flavor than those transported from another hemisphere. A medley of frozen vegetables can add variety to your diet, as well; rather than coping with a whole head of cauliflower, you can have just a taste in a "California blend."

Cooking vegetables: the basics

Boil

Fill a saucepan with enough water to cover the vegetable. Bring the water to a boil, add the vegetable, and cook to the desired tenderness. Drain and season.

Steam

Fill a steamer or saucepan with half an inch of water. Place the vegetable in the steamer insert or basket inside the pan. Bring the water to a boil. Reduce the heat to medium, cover, and cook to the desired tenderness.

Microwave

Pour a small amount of water or broth into a microwaveable container. Add the vegetable, season, and cover. Microwave the vegetable at full strength, checking often, to the desired tenderness. An ear of corn or whole potato can be wrapped in a damp paper towel and microwaved without additional water; husk the corn first, and pierce the potato with a knife to allow steam to escape.

Roast

Slice the vegetable and toss with oil and seasonings. Roast in a single layer, uncovered, at 400°F to 450°F. Some vegetables, such as eggplant and beets, can be pierced in several places and roasted unpeeled and whole.

Sauté

Heat a little oil or butter in a skillet set over medium to medium-high heat. Cook the vegetable, stirring often, to the desired tenderness. Fibrous vegetables, such as green beans and large asparagus, should be blanched (boiled briefly) before sautéing.

Easy ways to get your veggies

• Top cottage cheese with chopped raw vegetables such as tomatoes, carrots, radishes, and scallions. Sprinkle with a seasoning blend or freshly ground black pepper.

• Mix salsa with plain yogurt or reduced-fat sour cream to make a quick dip for raw vegetables such as carrot sticks, celery, baby carrots, Belgian endive, or the crisp inner leaves of romaine.

• Boil fresh or frozen edamame (unshelled soybeans) in salted water for 30 seconds to 1 minute. Shell and eat.

• Remove the tough bottom leaves of an artichoke; cut off the spiny top and most of the stem; peel the remaining stem. Steam the artichoke (see page 144) until an outer leaf can be pulled free easily. Savor with a dipping sauce of vinaigrette or butter and lemon juice.

• Choose baby spinach packaged for microwaving in the bag. Follow cooking directions on package, then transfer the microwaved spinach to a plate and season with butter, salt, and pepper.

• When your pasta water comes to a boil, drop in a serving of green beans or Brussels sprouts. When tender, scoop out the vegetable with a skimmer or slotted spoon, then cook pasta as usual.

Roasted Ratatouille

The vegetables in this recipe are those used traditionally in ratatouille, but here they're roasted—speedier than the traditional sauté-and-simmer method. Enjoy the ratatouille hot or at room temperature, alone or in other ways: as a salad, on a sandwich, as an omelet filling, on a pizza, or mixed with cooked pasta.

1 small eggplant, cut into 1-inch chunks

1 medium zucchini or yellow summer squash, cut into 1-inch chunks

1 small bell pepper (any color), stemmed and seeded, cut into 1-inch pieces

1 small onion, cut into thin wedges

1/4 cup olive oil

1/2 teaspoon herbes de Provence, fines herbes (see Note), or dried thyme leaves

Salt and freshly ground black pepper, to taste

1 small tomato, diced

1 teaspoon chopped garlic

1 Preheat the oven to 450°F. Spread the eggplant, zucchini, bell pepper, and onion in a single layer on a rimmed baking sheet. Drizzle the oil over the vegetables and sprinkle with the herbes de Provence, and salt and pepper to taste. Using your hands or a wooden spoon, mix the vegetables with the oil and seasonings until lightly coated.

2 Roast the vegetables, stirring occasionally, until lightly browned, about 20 minutes. Stir in the tomato and garlic, and cook 5 minutes longer.

VEGETABLES

Cook's Notes

—Herbes de Provence is a blend of Mediterranean herbs that includes rosemary, marjoram, thyme, and savory; fines herbes usually contains chervil, chives, parsley, and tarragon. Both are nice to have on hand to season soup, chicken, meat, etc.

—Allow a lot of room for the vegetables in the pan—otherwise they will steam rather than roast.

MAKES 1 (MAIN DISH) OR 2 (SIDE DISH) SERVINGS
PREP: 10 MINUTES
COOK: 8 MINUTES

Succulent Succotash

We have the Algonquin Indians to thank for the word succotash. Though this dish usually contains squash, peppers, and beans, the Native American word actually refers only to the corn. This bit of knowledge pleases me, because it seems to justify throwing just about anything good together with fresh corn. Succotash tastes great with a steak or softshell crab, but it's equally delicious as a light meal on its own.

2 teaspoons butter

1/2 cup diced zucchini

1/4 cup diced green bell pepper

1 small scallion with some of the green part, thinly sliced

1 ear fresh corn, husked

1 plum tomato, chopped

Salt and freshly ground black pepper, to taste

1 Melt the butter in a medium saucepan over medium heat. Add the zucchini, bell pepper, and scallion; cook, stirring occasionally, until lightly browned.

2 Meanwhile, holding the ear of corn upright on a cutting board, cut off the kernels with a serrated knife. Stir the corn and tomato into the vegetable mixture. Season to taste with salt and pepper. Reduce heat to low, cover, and cook a few minutes longer until the tomato is soft and the corn is hot.

MAKES 1 SERVING
PREP: 5 MINUTES
COOK: 5 MINUTES

Grilled Chile Relleno

This little vegetarian number can stand on its own as an entrée, perhaps paired with a baked potato, or you could grill a steak or chicken breast to go with it.

1 large poblano chile or Italian frying pepper (about 5 inches long), cut in half lengthwise, seeds removed

2 slices tomato, halved

4 thin slices pepper-Jack, cheddar, or other flavorful cheese

1 Preheat the grill to medium-hot. Place the chile pieces skin side up on the grill. Cook until lightly browned along the edges, about 3 minutes.

2 Turn the pieces and top with tomato and cheese slices. Cover and grill until the peppers soften and brown on the bottom and the cheese melts.

Pan-Seared Portabellas

I love this high-heat method of cooking mushrooms, which calls for adding chopped garlic at the end, cooking it just long enough to take off the edge. The portabellas are delicious on their own, or you can pile the slices on a bun, along with burger fixings.

2 small portabella mushroom caps (about 4 ounces total) (see Note)

1 teaspoon grapeseed oil or other vegetable oil

1 pinch salt

1/2 teaspoon finely chopped garlic

1/2 teaspoon sherry vinegar or balsamic vinegar

Freshly ground black pepper, to taste

1 Cut the portabellas into thick slices. Heat the oil in a medium skillet over high heat. Sprinkle the salt over the surface of the skillet and spread out the mushroom slices. Cook for a couple of minutes, stirring once or twice, until the slices soften and turn brown.

2 Remove the skillet from the heat and immediately add the garlic, stirring until the mushrooms stop sizzling. Sprinkle with the vinegar, and season to taste with pepper.

Cook's Note

You can substitute a comparable quantity of other fresh mushrooms for the portabellas—white button mushrooms, cremini, shiitakes, or, one of my favorites, hen of the woods mushrooms.

VEGETABLES

Southern-Fried Okra

My Texas roots show in my affection for fried okra. In our family, Aunt Pattie is the okra queen, but when I want to fry up a small batch for myself, I know how.

2 tablespoons all-purpose flour

2 tablespoons yellow cornmeal or instant polenta

1/4 teaspoon salt, plus more to taste

5 ounces fresh okra, trimmed and cut into 1/2-inch slices (about 1 cup)

2 tablespoons grapeseed oil or other vegetable oil, plus more as needed

1/2 small onion, thinly sliced

Freshly ground black pepper, to taste

1 Combine the flour, cornmeal, and 1/4 teaspoon salt in a shallow bowl. Add the okra and, using your fingers, mix until well coated.

2 Heat 2 tablespoons oil in a medium skillet (preferably cast iron) over medium heat. Toss in a sample piece of okra; when it sizzles, add the rest in a single layer. Cook, stirring occasionally, until the okra begins to change color, adding more oil only if necessary. Stir in the onion and continue to cook until it is tender and the okra is lightly browned (see Notes). Season to taste with more salt, if needed, and pepper.

Cook's Notes

—You should know that okra is, like eggplant, a glutton for oil. The trick is to give it enough to brown properly but not so much that it's oily tasting.

—Some people like their okra totally browned and crisp. I prefer to stop when the okra has a hybrid consistency—crisp and brown in places, green and yielding in others. It's all a matter of taste.

VEGETABLES

151

MAKES 1 SERVING
PREP: 5 MINUTES
COOK: 15 MINUTES

Creamy Smashed Potatoes

Smashing is the answer to a lazy cook's prayers: no peeling potatoes or striving for smoothness. You don't have to use half-and-half (milk is an acceptable substitute), but I'm never sorry when I do.

1 large or 2 small red-skinned potatoes (about 8 ounces)
1/2 teaspoon salt, plus more to taste
1 teaspoon butter
3 tablespoons half-and-half
1 scallion, chopped
Freshly ground black pepper, to taste

1 Quarter the potato and place in a small saucepan. Cover with water; add 1/2 teaspoon salt, and bring to a boil. Reduce the heat and simmer, covered, until very tender. Drain well.

2 Return the still-hot potato to the pan and smash with a potato masher or the end of a wooden spoon until broken into small chunks. Add the butter and, when it is incorporated, the half-and-half. Over low heat, continue to smash and stir the potato until fairly smooth. Add the scallion and season to taste with salt and pepper.

Spicy Corn on the Cob

When local corn is out of season, you can usually buy super-sweet varieties grown in the southern states. Refrigerated, the corn will stay sweet for several days, at least.

1 teaspoon mayonnaise or softened butter

1 ear fresh corn, husked

1/8–1/4 teaspoon Southwest or Cajun seasoning (see Note)

1 lime wedge

1 Heat a medium skillet over medium heat. Meanwhile, rub mayonnaise over the ear of corn, and sprinkle with the seasoning.

2 Place the corn in the skillet and cook, turning the ear with tongs as the kernels take on a brown, glazed look. Rub the lime wedge over the corn, squeezing out the juice.

Cook's Note

Most likely, the Southwest seasoning contains salt. If not, sprinkle a little over the corn.

Variation

Herbed Corn on the Cob: In place of mayonnaise or butter, rub the corn with olive oil. Sprinkle with salt and dried thyme, oregano, or Italian seasoning. Squeeze lemon juice over the cooked corn.

VEGETABLES

153

Swiss Chard, Good and Garlicky

If you're not familiar with Swiss chard, it's a lot like spinach, only better. Many recipes call for cooking the leaves only and saving the tougher stems for another purpose. Following the method described here, you can enjoy the contrasting texture of the toothsome stems and tender leaves. Finished with butter-browned garlic and a touch of vinegar, this chard is insanely good. Eat half hot and the rest chilled the next day.

1 small bunch Swiss chard

2 teaspoons butter

1–2 cloves garlic, thinly sliced

Salt and freshly ground black pepper, to taste

Good balsamic vinegar or white wine vinegar

1 Cut off the chard stems (see Note); wash the leaves and stems in several changes of water. Cut the stems crosswise into small pieces. Gathering several leaves at a time into a clump, cut crosswise into thin strips.

2 Meanwhile, bring a quart of water to a boil in a large saucepan. Add the stems, reduce heat to medium and simmer until tender, about 2 minutes. Add the shredded leaves and cook until soft, a minute or so longer.

3 Drain the chard. In the same saucepan, melt the butter. Cook the garlic in the butter, stirring, until golden but not burned (don't walk away!). Return the chard stems and leaves to the saucepan, and stir until well coated with the butter mixture. Season to taste with salt and pepper, and drizzle with a little vinegar just before eating.

Cook's Note

Choose chard with slender stems about 1/2 inch thick; the red-stemmed kind is just plain prettier. Fold the leaves away from the stem and make a V-shaped incision to remove the stem.

MAKES 1 SERVING
PREP: 5 MINUTES
COOK: 3 MINUTES

Steamed Asparagus

Capers add a pleasantly piquant note to steamed asparagus.

4–6 stalks asparagus

1/2–1 teaspoon capers

2 teaspoons extra-virgin olive oil

Salt and freshly ground black pepper, to taste

1 Trim the ends of the asparagus stalks (see Note) and angle-cut into 2-inch pieces.

2 Bring 1/2 inch water to a boil in a steamer or saucepan fitted with a steamer insert. Place the asparagus and capers in the steamer and cook, covered, until the asparagus is crisp-tender. Transfer to a dinner plate and toss gently with olive oil; add salt and pepper to taste.

Cook's Note

There's more than one way to trim asparagus, but one of the nicest is to peel the bottom half of the stalks with a vegetable peeler, then snap off the tough ends.

MAKES 1 SERVING
PREP: 2 MINUTES
COOK: 5 MINUTES

Broccoli with Hazelnuts

Hazelnuts make steamed broccoli just a little bit special.

1 small broccoli crown, trimmed

2 teaspoons butter

1 heaping tablespoon chopped roasted, blanched hazelnuts, or walnuts (see Note)

Salt and freshly ground black pepper, to taste

1 Cut off the broccoli florets, separating them; cut the stem into smaller pieces. Bring 1/2 inch water to a boil in a steamer or saucepan fitted with a steamer insert; reduce heat to medium. Place the broccoli in the steamer and cook, covered, until just tender, about 4 minutes.

2 Transfer the broccoli to a bowl and discard the steaming water. Melt the butter in the same saucepan and, when it sizzles, stir in the hazelnuts. Add the broccoli, turning it to coat with butter, and season to taste with salt and pepper.

Cook's Note

If you can't find roasted hazelnuts, crisp raw ones by cooking them a little longer in the butter. Either way, buy hazelnuts that are blanched (skins removed). Chopped walnuts that don't need roasting can be substituted.

pizza

Tips for Pizza-Making Success

Pizza Presto

Traditional Pizzas

- Basic Pizza Dough
- Pizza Margherita
- White Pizza with Sausage and Mushrooms
- Roast Potato and Pesto Pizza

More Great Pies

- Eggplant-Hummus Pizza
- Chicken, Spinach, and Blue Cheese Pizza
- Grilled Pizza with Brie and Arugula
- Ricotta-Salami Calzone

Pizza is a delicious and surprisingly easy dinner to make just for yourself. Trying to turn out the same thing your local pizzeria delivers is not the point. Instead, this is a chance to use superior ingredients, to try an unusual combination such as a potato and pesto topping, or to invent your own.

There are many options for personal-size pizza crusts. You can make dough for several solo pizzas, following the recipe in this chapter. Most supermarkets carry uncooked pizza dough—in a bag or rolled out, fresh or frozen—and some mom-and-pop pizzerias will sell a pound of pizza dough at a modest cost.

A fully cooked crust is even more convenient. I like to use flatbread such as naan (an Indian bread) or pocketless pitas or, for a thin, cracker-like crust, split a regular pita and top each half. A bagel or bialy makes a good pizza base. Some prebaked pizza crusts, such as Boboli, have onions, olive oil, and Italian cheeses already cooked into them. A flour tortilla is yet another option.

As for toppings, it's hard to think of something that *can't* go on a pizza crust. Some ideas to try:

Make a white pie by skipping the tomato base and covering the crust instead with seasoned ricotta, grated mozzarella, or another cheese.

Search your refrigerator for chop-and-top tidbits such as the last slice of Italian salami, a marinated artichoke heart or two, a few olives, or leftover cooked spinach or broccoli.

Create a "salad pizza" by scattering greens tossed with a piquant dressing over any cooked pie.

Check your seasoning and condiment shelves for pizza enhancers such as garlic oil, crushed red pepper, oregano, and seasoning blends.

A final word of advice: Keep your pizza-making simple. A pizza overloaded with a "kitchen sink" topping is likely to be soggy and unappealing. Three or four ingredients that taste good together are enough.

Tips for pizza-making success

Getting ready

You can cook a small pizza on a round aluminum pizza pan or a rimmed baking sheet.

A pizza stone helps produce a crisp crust, but cheap, unglazed quarry tiles are equally effective. They are available at home improvement and tile stores. Buy enough to line an oven shelf plus a few extras to allow for breakage. When not in use, they stack compactly in the back of a cabinet. If you don't have a pizza stone or tiles and don't feel like acquiring them, you can make a good pizza anyway.

About toppings

Ideally, the topping finishes cooking at the same time as the crust. For cheeses, cured meats such as pepperoni, and tomato sauce, the timing works out fine whether you put them on an uncooked or cooked pizza crust.

Other ingredients do better when partly cooked ahead of time. Sautéing or roasting onions, peppers, and mushrooms reduces their bulk, eliminates excess moisture that could turn the crust soggy, and adds a protective coating of oil.

Thawing pizza dough

Move the dough from the freezer to the refrigerator the day before you plan to use it, or thaw at room temperature for a couple of hours.

Shaping and baking

Place the ball of dough on a lightly oiled pan. Gently press and stretch the dough to form a crust eight to nine inches in diameter.

If you're using tiles or a pizza stone, arrange them on a rack in the middle of a cold oven, then preheat to 450°F. Place your pizza pan on top of the tiles when oven is hot, or slide an unbaked or partially baked pizza directly onto the tiles.

The amount of baking time may vary a bit, depending on the toppings, but typically it's about eight minutes for a prebaked crust and fifteen minutes for one that's not.

Toaster oven tips

Shape the dough or cut a prebaked crust to fit if you want to cook your pizza in a toaster oven. Set the baking/roasting temperature at 450°F, and place the pizza directly on the rack.

For reheating pizza, a toaster oven is far superior to a microwave, crisping the crust rather than toughening it.

Pizza Presto

To make an appetizing solo pizza in almost no time, rely on condiments and leftover tidbits in your refrigerator. Until now, you may not have imagined that the moo-shu mixture sitting in a Chinese takeout carton in your refrigerator could be the key ingredient in a solo pizza. Leftover vegetables and cold cuts are equally promising.

Here are a few suggestions for inventive pizzas:

Better than plain

Spread 1/4 cup marinara sauce on an uncooked or fully cooked crust. Add one or more toppings: 1/2 teaspoon minced garlic, 2 sliced artichoke hearts, 2 sliced pitted olives, 3 quartered pepperoni slices, 1/4 cup drained, canned clams or crabmeat. Optional: 1 tablespoon freshly grated cheese such as Pecorino Romano. Bake in a preheated 425°F oven for ten to fifteen minutes.

Moo-shu special

Brush a few drops of sesame oil or chili oil on an uncooked or fully cooked crust. Spread with 1 to 2 tablespoons hoisin sauce. Arrange 1/2 to 3/4 cup pork, shrimp, or vegetarian moo-shu on top. Brush the top with a few drops of sesame oil or chili oil. Bake in a preheated 425°F oven for ten to fifteen minutes.

Cheese pizza, vegetized

Saute 1/2 cup sliced onion with 1/2 cup sliced yellow squash, bell pepper, or mushrooms in a little olive oil until soft and lightly browned. Season with salt and, if you like, crushed red pepper. Spread the mixture over a large slice of purchased cheese pizza. If the pizza is already hot, you're ready to eat. Otherwise, heat the vegetable-topped pizza in a preheated 425°F oven.

Basic Pizza Dough

This recipe makes enough dough for several single-portion pizzas—one to eat now and the others for later.

1 envelope (2 + 1/2 teaspoons) yeast (see Note)
2 tablespoons extra-virgin olive oil, plus more for bowl
2 + 1/2 cups unbleached all-purpose flour, plus more for dusting
1 teaspoon salt

1 Sprinkle the yeast over 1 cup warm water (110° to 115°F), and shake gently to moisten it. When a thin layer of scum forms on top, indicating that the yeast is active, stir in 2 tablespoons olive oil.

2 Mix 2 cups of the flour with the salt in a large mixing bowl. Stir in the yeast mixture. Once the liquid is incorporated, turn the dough onto a floured pastry or cutting board. Knead for about 5 minutes, adding up to 1/2 cup additional flour as necessary, until the dough is soft but elastic and only slightly sticky.

3 Divide the dough into 3 pieces and form into balls. Clean and dry the mixing bowl, and lightly coat the inside with olive oil. Turn one ball of dough in the bowl to coat it with oil and cover the top with plastic wrap. Place each of the other balls in a 1-quart resealable plastic bag, or double wrap in plastic wrap; refrigerate for up to 2 days or freeze.

4 Allow the dough in the bowl to rise at room temperature until doubled in bulk, 1 to 1 + 1/2 hours; if you are making the dough several hours in advance, refrigerate it. (See page 162 for directions on shaping and baking the dough once it rises.)

Cook's Note

If you use quick-rising yeast, the dough will be ready to use in 45 minutes or less.

MAKES 1 SOLO PIZZA
PREP: 10 MINUTES
COOK: 15 MINUTES

Pizza Margherita

This is one of the most basic—and most popular—of pizzas, and how it comes out depends enormously on the quality of the ingredients. If you take a little trouble over making or choosing them, you'll be rewarded with a wonderful pizza.

Extra-virgin olive oil

6 ounces store-bought or homemade pizza dough (page 164)

1/2 cup roughly chopped fresh or canned plum tomatoes

2 tablespoons thinly sliced basil leaves (see Note)

1/2 cup grated fresh mozzarella cheese

1 slice prosciutto di Parma (optional)

1 Preheat the oven to 450°F. Lightly brush a pizza pan or rimmed baking sheet with olive oil; roll or pat the dough into a round about 8 inches in diameter (see directions on page 162). Transfer the dough to the prepared pan; lightly brush with olive oil.

2 Spread tomatoes over the crust, leaving a 1/2-inch border around the edge. Scatter half of the basil on top, then sprinkle with mozzarella.

3 Bake the pizza until the crust is crisp and the cheese melts, about 15 minutes. Tear the prosciutto di Parma (if using) into several smaller pieces and scatter over the hot pizza.

Cook's Notes

—To cut the basil into ribbons, stack several leaves and roll from one of the long sides to make a cylinder; cut crosswise.

—You can substitute a prebaked crust (6 to 8 inches) for the dough. Skip brushing oil on the pan and crust. The pizza will be ready in 10 minutes.

—You can also substitute 1/3 cup marinara sauce for the tomatoes.

White Pizza with Sausage and Mushrooms

I like this pizza because the robust flavors of the mushrooms and sausage come through more than when the crust is slathered with the usual tomato sauce.

1 teaspoon extra-virgin olive oil, plus more for the pan

6 ounces store-bought or homemade pizza dough (page 164), or 1 fully cooked crust (6–8 inches)

1/2 hot or sweet Italian sausage (about 4 ounces)

3 white or cremini mushrooms, thinly sliced (about 2/3 cup)

1/4 cup diced red or yellow bell pepper (optional)

Pinch of salt

1/2 cup grated Fontina or Gruyère cheese

1 Preheat the oven to 450°F. Lightly brush a pizza pan or rimmed baking sheet with olive oil; gently stretch the dough into a round, 8 to 9 inches in diameter (see directions on page 162); lightly brush with olive oil. (If using a fully baked crust, simply place it on an ungreased pan.)

2 Heat 1 teaspoon olive oil in a medium skillet over medium heat. Squeeze the sausage out of the casing into the skillet, breaking it up with a wooden spoon. When it loses its raw look, after about 2 minutes, add the mushrooms, bell pepper (if using), and salt. Cook, stirring often, until the mushrooms soften and begin to brown, about 3 minutes.

3 Sprinkle the cheese evenly over the crust, and arrange the sausage-mushroom mixture on top. Bake the pizza until the bottom crust and the topping are browned, about 15 minutes (a prebaked crust will take only about 8 minutes).

Vegetarian Version

Leave out the sausage, and double the quantity of mushrooms. For a little extra punch, season the sautéed mushrooms with crushed red pepper.

Roast Potato and Pesto Pizza

Potato pizza? It's not an idiosyncratic combination but an Italian classic that I've made ever since running across it twenty years ago in a cookbook called *Chez Panisse Pasta, Pizza, and Calzone* by Alice Waters. The perfect go-along: ripe tomato slices.

Extra-virgin olive oil

1 medium red-skinned potato, sliced into 1/4-inch rounds

6 ounces store-bought or homemade pizza dough (page 164)

3 teaspoons plus 1 teaspoon store-bought or homemade pesto (page 88)

1 Preheat the oven to 450°F. Cover the bottom of a roasting pan or other shallow pan with aluminum foil. Lightly brush olive oil on a pizza pan or rimmed baking sheet.

2 Arrange the potato slices in a single layer on the foil-lined pan. Roast until barely tender, about 10 minutes.

3 Meanwhile, place the dough on the pizza pan. Gently stretch it into a round about 8 inches in diameter (see directions on page 162). Brush the crust with 3 teaspoons of the pesto. Arrange the potato slices on top and brush with the remaining pesto.

4 Cook the pizza until the crust and topping are browned, 15 to 17 minutes.

Cook's Note

Even better: After baking the pizza, brush the potato slices with a little more pesto.

MAKES 1 SOLO PIZZA
PREP: 10 MINUTES
COOK: 20 MINUTES

Eggplant-Hummus Pizza

These familiar Mediterranean flavors are right at home on a flatbread pizza.

1 small Italian or Japanese eggplant, trimmed (about 4 ounces)

Extra-virgin olive oil

Salt

1/3 cup homemade hummus (page 211) or any flavor prepared hummus

1 oblong (6 by 4 inches) or round naan or pocketless pita

2–3 tablespoons crumbled feta cheese

1 Preheat the oven to 450°F. Cut the eggplant crosswise into 1/4-inch slices. Arrange the slices in a single layer on a pizza pan or rimmed baking sheet. Lightly brush both sides with oil and sprinkle with salt.

2 Roast the eggplant until lightly browned on both sides, about 10 minutes total, turning once. Meanwhile, spread the hummus on the naan.

3 Arrange the eggplant slices on top of the hummus. Sprinkle with the feta cheese. Bake until the naan is crisp and the topping is heated through, about 10 minutes.

Cook's Note

This pizza is an especially good candidate for the toaster oven, especially when made with an oblong naan, which fits neatly on the rack.

Chicken, Spinach, and Blue Cheese Pizza

This is what you could call a square-meal pizza, complete with a protein source (chicken) and a green vegetable (spinach).

1 teaspoon extra-virgin olive oil, plus more for the pan

1 small chicken breast cutlet (about 3 ounces), cut into strips

1/4 cup sliced shallot or onion

3/4 cup frozen cut leaf spinach from a bag, thawed (see Note)

Salt and freshly ground black pepper, to taste

1 (7-inch) pocketless pita

2 tablespoons crumbled blue cheese (such as Roquefort or Gorgonzola)

1 Preheat the oven to 450°F. Heat 1 teaspoon olive oil in a medium skillet over medium heat. Cook the chicken and shallot, stirring constantly, until just cooked, about 2 minutes. Stir in the spinach and cook a few seconds longer. Season with salt and pepper.

2 Place the pita on a pizza pan or baking sheet. Spread the chicken-spinach mixture over the pita and scatter the blue cheese on top. Bake until the crust is crisp and the cheese melts, about 8 minutes.

Cook's Note

For the frozen spinach, you can substitute 1 cup roughly chopped fresh spinach leaves. After adding to the chicken mixture, cook just until wilted.

MAKES 1 SOLO PIZZA
PREP: 10 MINUTES
COOK: 10 MINUTES

Grilled Pizza with Brie and Arugula

If you have a grill and like firing it up, try grilling pizza. You'll be rewarded with a very crisp crust and enjoyable grilled flavor.

Extra-virgin olive oil

6 ounces store-bought or homemade pizza dough (page 164)

1 cup baby arugula or torn arugula leaves

1/4 teaspoon balsamic vinegar

Salt, to taste

3–4 tomato slices

2–3 ounces Brie or Camembert cheese, sliced

2–3 pitted green Spanish olives, or garlic-stuffed "martini olives," sliced

1 Preheat the grill to high. Lightly brush a pizza pan or rimmed baking sheet with olive oil; place the dough in the center and gently stretch it into an oblong shape (see directions on page 162). In a small bowl, toss the arugula with the vinegar and salt.

2 Grill the tomato slices, turning once (see Note). Once they soften, after a couple of minutes, transfer with a spatula to a plate. Holding the dough with both hands, lay it directly on the grill (don't worry if it looks a little misshapen). Cook until it hardens and grill marks form, about 3 minutes; turn and grill the other side, checking the bottom to make sure it doesn't burn. Transfer to a plate.

3 Distribute cheese slices over the crust. Top with tomato and olives. Grill just until the cheese melts and the bottom is crisp. Transfer to a plate and top with the dressed arugula leaves.

Cook's Notes

—Cook the tomatoes on a vegetable grate if you have one. And while you're at it, grill a couple of onion slices (not recommended for a regular rack because they tend to fall through).

—Whether you cut the rind off the Brie is a matter of personal taste. It's edible, so I leave it on. You can also use spreadable Brie, with the rind already removed, available in a plastic tub.

—You can substitute a 7-inch Boboli or other fully cooked crust for the pizza dough. It will take a little less time to crisp.

Ricotta-Salami Calzone

Extra-virgin olive oil

6 ounces pizza dough, store-bought or homemade (page 164)

1/2 cup ricotta

2 tablespoons coarsely chopped Genoa salami or soppressata

**1 tablespoon grated Pecorino Romano or Parmigiano-Reggiano
  cheese**

1 tablespoon chopped flat-leaf parsley or baby spinach (optional)

Pinch freshly ground black or white pepper

1 Preheat the oven to 450°F. Lightly brush a pizza pan or baking sheet with olive oil; place the dough on the pan and gently stretch it into a circular shape about 7 inches in diameter (see directions on page 162).

2 In a small bowl, mix the ricotta, salami, cheese, parsley (if using), and pepper with a fork. Spread the mixture over half of the pizza dough, leaving a 1/2-inch border. Fold the other half over and press the edges together.

3 Bake for 10 minutes. Slide the calzone off the pan and onto the oven rack. Continue cooking until browned, about 5 minutes longer.

<u>Cook's Notes</u>

—If your supermarket carries it, buy all-natural ricotta, which tastes creamier and less gelatinous than other varieties. As for the leftover ricotta, it's terrific spread on toast with marmalade or fruit preserves on top.

—If you like, double the quantities and make two calzones. After the extra one cools, wrap it and refrigerate. Reheat the next day in an oven or toaster oven set on low.

<u>Variation</u>

Ricotta-Olive Calzone: For the salami, substitute 2 tablespoons chopped pitted Kalamata or other flavorful olives.

sandwiches & tortillas

Fresh Sandwich Ideas

Breads and Spreads

Warm Sandwiches

- Pressed Muenster and Avocado Sandwich

- Bulgogi on a Bun

- Open-Face Curry Burger

'wiches to Chill with

- Muffaletta, Sorta

- Bagel with Smoked Salmon

- Crostini with Goat Cheese–Tomato Topping

- Smoked Turkey Wrap

Tortilla Creations

- Shrimp Fajitas

- Refried Bean Tostadas

- Sautéed Veggie Quesadilla

Sandwiches can be light or filling. Cold or hot. Open-faced or not. Portable or knife-and-fork fare. Familiar, imaginative, or downright strange. Most often, it's the quality of the ingredients that separates an ordinary sandwich from a great one. Take that old standby, the BLT. Fry some hand-sliced, apple-smoked bacon from a good deli, add ripe tomato slices and tender Boston lettuce leaves, pile it all on toasted challah bread with a smear of mayo, and you've got a sandwich to remember.

Improvisations are a sandwich-making tradition, but it's easy to get in a rut. The recipes and ideas given here will help set you free of the same old—same old syndrome. Instead of your usual turkey on whole-wheat, good as that is, try something new. Indulge in a spicy muffaletta, for instance, or bulgogi on a bun. Wraps, made with a flour tortilla or the Middle Eastern flatbread called lavash, are yet another kind of sandwich. And, like sandwiches, tortilla creations such as quesadillas and tostadas offer an opportunity to experiment with whatever ingredient combinations strike your fancy.

Fresh sandwich ideas

Breads, fillings, and condiments can be fashioned into an infinite number of satisfying sandwiches. This realization was brought home to me by a hungry teenage nephew who, after a brief but purposeful rummage through our refrigerator, improvised a burrito of cold roast pork and salsa. You may have the makings of a splendid sandwich right in your kitchen! Invent something, or try a few of these combinations.

Proportions are up to you, but in general allow four to five ounces of cold cuts or other fillings per sandwich.

Tuna trio

● **Tuna niçoise:** Toss oil-packed canned tuna (preferably from Italy or Spain), pitted niçoise or other good-tasting olives, capers, and chopped roasted red pepper in store-bought or homemade vinaigrette. Spoon onto a sandwich roll and finish with a handful of mixed greens.

● **Tuna-artichoke:** Dice leftover grilled tuna and mix with quartered artichoke hearts, chopped scallions, mayonnaise, and a little Dijon mustard. Eat on seven-grain bread.

● **Waldorf tuna:** Mix canned tuna with chopped apple, celery, walnuts, mayo, and ground pepper. Pile the filling on oatmeal bread.

Panini with panache

● **Cheese:** Split a square of focaccia and brush the cut sides with vinaigrette. Lay thick slices of Scamorza (smoked mozzarella) or Fontina on one half. Top with arugula leaves and close the sandwich.

● **Mushroom:** Spread a sesame bun with mayo and/or Dijon mustard, and fill with sautéed sliced mushrooms or pan-seared portabellas (page 150), plus some shredded lettuce.

● **Salmon and cucumber:** Spread thin slices of pumpernickel bread with chive-flavored cream cheese. Add layers of smoked salmon and thin cucumber slices.

● **Mixed vegetable grill:** On a hero roll, place some roasted vegetables from a deli or Roasted Ratatouille (page 146), drizzling some of the juices on the bread. Add a couple of thin fresh mozzarella slices.

● **Roast beef:** Spread country-style white bread with a mixture of softened butter and Gorgonzola cheese. Between the slices, layer roast beef shavings and watercress sprigs.

- **Sardine:** Make an open-face sandwich of canned sardines, arugula, and sweet onion slices on pumpernickel or rye bread spread with hot mustard or horseradish sauce.

Classic Variations

- **Bratwurst:** Split a long bun and spread with Dijon mustard, put a hot brat in the middle, and cover with thin slivers of Muenster cheese; heat in a toaster oven or under a broiler long enough to melt the cheese. (For the brat, you can substitute knockwurst or any other fully cooked sausage.)

- **Egg:** Tuck a Mexican-style scramble (page 196) into whole-wheat pita halves, along with mixed greens.

- **Curried chicken:** Combine leftover shredded or diced chicken with chopped apple, onion, and a dollop of curry-sprinkled mayonnaise. Enjoy it on raisin-walnut bread.

- **Chile-cheese:** Cover 2 pieces of whole-wheat bread with slices of pepper-Jack cheese; put a layer of alfalfa sprouts in the middle, and toast in a greased skillet or toaster oven until the cheese melts.

Breads

Look for hard rolls and other sandwich breads sold by the piece. When you buy more than you will need in the immediate future, wrap some of it securely in plastic wrap and freeze; keep the rest, well wrapped, at room temperature.

Rather than automatically reaching for your usual white or whole wheat bread, try a marbled sourdough loaf, a seven-grain bread, or one of these alternatives, ideal for sandwich making:

● **Hard sandwich roll:** taste and texture of a baguette in a manageable size; sourdough is even better

● **Croissant:** soft texture and delicate, buttery taste

● **Ficelle:** like a baguette but skinnier; pumpernickel variety is worth a try

● **Focaccia:** pizzalike texture and taste; split for sandwich making; try seasoned versions such as rosemary

● **Lavash:** soft Middle Eastern flatbread; use for wraps as an alternative to flour tortillas

● **Pita:** comes in mini and full sizes, regular and pocketless; try variations such as onion and whole wheat

...and Spreads

Sandwich spreads and sauces keep bread from drying out and bind chopped fillings that might otherwise fall out. Ideally, they should add another flavor dimension.

● To perk up plain mayonnaise, add a sprinkle of curry powder or ground red pepper, a pinch of grated ginger or a squeeze of lemon juice.

● Drizzle or brush extra-virgin olive oil or Basic Vinaigrette (page 32) onto a crusty European-style bread.

● Leave bland ballpark mustard on the supermarket shelf. Instead, choose a grainy Dijon or honey mustard.

● Spoon on dabs of salsa to enliven a sandwich.

● Try a fruit sauce, such as ginger-peach chutney or whole cranberry sauce, on sandwiches filled with roast or grilled meats.

● Spread pita, lavash, and other flatbreads with hummus. Buy a good brand or mix up a batch of homemade hummus (page 211).

Pressed Muenster and Avocado Sandwich

If you own one of the countertop panini presses now on the market, use it to make this delicious sandwich. Otherwise, follow the method described here.

2 slices 7-grain or sourdough bread

2 tablespoons store-bought or homemade (page 211) hummus

1 tablespoon Dijon mustard

2–4 thin slices Muenster, Monterey Jack, or pepper-Jack cheese (about 2 ounces)

1/4 peeled, pitted Hass avocado

1 slice red onion, rings separated

2 slices tomato

1 teaspoon olive oil

1 Spread one slice of bread with the hummus and the other with the mustard. Layer the cheese, avocado, onion, and tomato on the hummus side. Top with the other slice, and press firmly on the sandwich to fix the ingredients in place.

2 In a small skillet, heat the oil over medium-low heat. Place the sandwich in the center, cover with a piece of aluminum foil and place a weight on top (see Note). Cook, peeking once or twice, until the underside is browned, about 5 minutes. Turn the sandwich, weight it in the same way, and cook a few minutes longer until the bread is browned and the cheese melted.

Cook's Notes

—The sandwich can be weighted with two plain unglazed tiles, stacked one on top of another, or a small heavy saucepan.

—The relatively low cooking temperature ensures that the bread doesn't brown before the inside of the sandwich is hot and melty.

Open-Face Variation

Preheat an oven or toaster oven to 400°F. Toast 1 slice of bread until crisp and brown. Spread with hummus or mustard, and layer with the toppings listed above, finishing with the cheese. Heat until the cheese melts. Eat with a knife and fork.

Bulgogi on a Bun

This recipe makes enough spicy marinated beef for two meals. You might refrigerate half of it to cook the next night, either prepared the same way or stir-fried with vegetables—sliced baby bok choy and mushrooms, for example.

8 ounces boneless beef sirloin, or another tender cut, partially frozen

1 tablespoon soy sauce

2 teaspoons toasted sesame oil

2 teaspoons mirin (Japanese sweet rice wine)

2 teaspoons sugar

1 small clove garlic, minced or pressed

1/8 teaspoon ground pepper

1 Kaiser roll or other soft sandwich roll, split

1/4 cup shredded radicchio

1 slice sweet onion

1 With a sharp knife, cut the beef against the grain into very thin slices, about 1/8 inch thick.

2 In a small bowl, combine the soy sauce, sesame oil, mirin, sugar, garlic, and pepper. Add the beef, turning it until well coated with the marinade. Let stand for 15 minutes. Place half the beef in a resealable plastic bag and refrigerate or freeze for another use.

3 Heat a skillet (preferably nonstick) over high heat. Cook the beef along with the marinade, turning the strips as they brown, until cooked through. Reduce the heat and add a little water to make the mixture a bit saucy.

4 Warm the bun in a toaster or toaster oven. Spoon the bulgogi on the bottom half, top with radicchio and onion, and place the other half on top.

Open-Face Curry Burger

This is a good recipe to double—cook one burger to eat now and freeze the other.

1 tablespoon finely chopped scallion or onion

1/8 teaspoon curry powder

1/8 teaspoon jarred Asian chili paste (sambal oelek) or 1 dash hot sauce

1/8 teaspoon salt

4 ounces ground beef, bison, or turkey

1 teaspoon grapeseed oil or other vegetable oil

Mango chutney, such as Major Grey's

1/2 piece naan (Indian flatbread) or 1/2 English muffin

1 In a small bowl, combine the scallion, curry powder, chili paste, and salt. Add the ground meat and, with a fork, gently mix with the seasonings. Use your hands to form a patty packed just enough to hold together.

2 Heat the oil in a small skillet over medium-high heat. Cook the burger until well browned, about 3 minutes. Flip it and fry until browned on the outside and cooked through or barely pink at the center, about 2 minutes longer.

3 Meanwhile, warm the naan briefly, or toast the English muffin half until crisp. Place the burger on the bread and top with chutney.

Variation

For a bunless burger, skip the bread and, if you like, wrap the burger in soft lettuce leaves.

Muffaletta, Sorta

This sandwich is based loosely on the New Orleans version of an overstuffed deli sandwich, in the same family as a hoagie or hero.

3–4 pickled hot or sweet pepper rings

3 pitted green or black olives, chopped

1 tablespoon extra-virgin olive oil

1 teaspoon white wine vinegar or balsamic vinegar

1 round sandwich roll such as a Kaiser, split

2 thin slices fresh or smoked mozzarella cheese (about 2 ounces)

4–5 slices Italian cured meats (about 2 ounces) (see Note)

Shredded lettuce

1 In a small bowl, combine the pepper rings, olives, olive oil, and vinegar. Tear some of the soft bread from the cut sides of the roll; discard or use for another purpose.

2 Spread the olive-pepper mixture on the cut sides of the roll. Top the bottom half with the cheese, meats, and lettuce. Place the other half of the roll on top.

Cook's Notes

—You can use jarred olives and pickled peppers or, better yet, buy a small quantity at a deli counter.

—A well-equipped deli will carry several kinds of Italian cured meats, including prosciutto di Parma, capacolla, soppressata, Genoa salami, and mortadella. For a more interesting sandwich, buy two kinds rather than one.

MAKES 1 SERVING
PREP: 5 MINUTES
COOK: 2 MINUTES

Bagel with Smoked Salmon

A bagel with smoked salmon and cream cheese is traditional weekend brunch fare, at least on the East Coast, but to me, this open-faced sandwich is also appealing at the lunch or dinner hour.

1 teaspoon capers, rinsed (optional)
1 fresh bagel (plain or rye) or bialy, split
1/4 cup soft cream cheese (see Note)
2 ounces smoked salmon
2 thin slices sweet onion
Freshly ground black pepper

1 If you're using capers, roughly chop them if they are large; if they're small, leave them whole.

2 Toast the bagel in a toaster or toaster oven. Spread the warm halves with the cream cheese. Press the capers into the cream cheese. Arrange the smoked salmon and onion slices on top. Add a grinding of pepper.

Cook's Notes

—For easier spreading, use whipped cream cheese.

—Substitute cream cheese with scallions or chives already mixed in for the plain cream cheese and onion slices.

—If you make this open-faced sandwich in advance for a brownbag lunch, don't toast the bagel.

MAKES 1 SERVING
PREP: 5 MINUTES
COOK: 5 MINUTES

Crostini with Goat Cheese–Tomato Topping

Rather than serving crostini to guests as an hors d'oeuvre, have your own party with several of these dainty open-face sandwiches and a glass of wine.

1/2 cup chopped tomato

1 teaspoon extra-virgin olive oil

1/2 teaspoon minced garlic

1/4 teaspoon capers, rinsed and chopped

1–2 pinches salt

4 thin slices bread from a baguette (see Note)

1–2 ounces goat cheese, at room temperature (3–4 tablespoons)

1 In a small bowl, combine the tomato, olive oil, garlic, capers, and salt. Let stand 15 minutes to 1 hour.

2 Toast the bread in a toaster or toaster oven on the light setting until crisp but not browned. Spread the warm crostini with goat cheese.

3 Using a slotted spoon to drain some of the juices, top the crostini with the tomato mixture.

Cook's Notes

—You can substitute bread from any country-style loaf—sourdough, whole-wheat, and olive would all be good choices.

—Save any leftover tomato mixture to spoon into an omelet or add to salad greens.

Smoked Turkey Wrap

Use this recipe as a model for inventing your own wraps.

1/2 cup store-bought cole slaw

1 (8-inch) flour tortilla

2–3 thin slices smoked turkey (about 2 ounces)

3 thin slices provolone or Monterey Jack cheese (about 2 ounces)

3 thin slices tomato

1 Spread the cole slaw on the tortilla, leaving a 1/2-inch border around the edges. Layer the turkey, cheese, and tomato on top.

2 Fold in two opposing edges of the tortilla and, starting at the adjacent edge nearest you, roll it tightly around the filling. Cut diagonally in half.

Cook's Note

Even better, sprinkle the filling with chopped hot or sweet pickled peppers.

MAKES 1 SERVING
PREP: 10 MINUTES
COOK: 5 MINUTES

Shrimp Fajitas

These seafood fajitas, with the lively flavors of cilantro and lime, make lighter eating than the meaty fajitas served in most Mexican restaurants.

2 teaspoons plus 1 teaspoon vegetable oil

1 small Italian frying pepper (or 1/2 small bell pepper), cut into narrow strips

4 thin slices onion

2 (8-inch) flour tortillas

8–10 medium shrimp, peeled and deveined

Salt

1 lime wedge

Leaves from 1 sprig cilantro (about 2 tablespoons)

Store-bought picante sauce or salsa

1 Heat 2 teaspoons of the oil in a medium skillet over medium-high heat. Stir-fry the pepper and onion until soft and slightly charred at the edges (take care they do not burn). Transfer to a plate.

2 Heat the remaining 1 teaspoon oil in the same skillet. Stir-fry the shrimp until they lose their raw look, about 30 seconds. Return the onion-pepper mixture to the skillet and remove from the heat. Sprinkle the shrimp and vegetables lightly with salt. Squeeze lime juice over the mixture and add the cilantro.

3 Meanwhile, warm each tortilla in a dry, hot skillet, turning once. Spoon half of the shrimp mixture down the center of each tortilla. Drizzle with picante sauce. Fold in 2 opposing edges of each tortilla and, starting with the adjacent edge nearest you, tightly roll the tortilla around the filling.

Refried Bean Tostadas

2/3 cup shredded romaine or iceberg lettuce

2 radishes, cut into matchsticks

2 teaspoons plus 1 teaspoon grapeseed oil or other vegetable oil

1 teaspoon lime juice

Pinch of salt

2 (4 + 1/2-inch) corn tortillas

1/4 cup refried beans (preferably "spicy nonfat")

2–3 tablespoons crumbled feta cheese or queso fresco

2 green or black olives, pitted and sliced

1 slice onion, rings separated

1 Combine the lettuce and radishes in a small bowl. Add 2 teaspoons of the oil, the lime juice, and the salt. Set aside.

2 Heat the remaining 1 teaspoon oil in a large skillet over medium heat. Fry the tortillas on both sides until crisp, about 5 minutes. Drain on a paper towel.

3 Spread refried beans on the tortillas. Top with the reserved salad mixture, cheese, olives, and onion.

Optional Add-Ons

cooked shredded or diced chicken, halved cherry tomatoes, avocado cubes, picante sauce

Sautéed Veggie Quesadilla

Quesadillas are often Latin in spirit, filled with refried beans, Monterey Jack cheese, salsa, and the like. I enjoy those flavors, but realized somewhere along the way that just about any filling tastes good between a pair of crisp, golden tortillas. Here's one that goes heavy on the veggies.

2 teaspoons plus 1 teaspoon extra-virgin olive oil

2 slices onion

3–4 asparagus spears, trimmed and cut into 1-inch pieces

1/2 small yellow squash, trimmed, and thinly sliced

Salt and freshly ground black pepper, to taste

2 tablespoons Boursin or other soft herbed cheese

2 (8-inch) flour tortillas

1 Heat 2 teaspoons of the oil in a medium skillet (preferably nonstick) over medium heat. Sauté the onion, stirring often, until tender, about 3 minutes. Add the asparagus and squash, and sauté several minutes longer until tender (see Note). Season to taste with salt and pepper. Scrape the vegetable mixture into a bowl, and rinse or wipe out the skillet.

2 Spread cheese on each tortilla. Spoon the vegetable mixture onto one tortilla, and top with the other, cheesy side down.

3 Heat the remaining 1 teaspoon oil in the same skillet over medium heat, smoothing it over the bottom of the skillet with a heatproof spatula. Cook the quesadilla until lightly browned. Turn and cook until browned on the other side and the filling is hot (see Note).

4 Let the quesadilla cool a bit, and cut into 4 wedges.

Cook's Notes

—Asparagus can be a little stubborn. If it's still firm after the other vegetables are done: Lower the heat, add a bit of water and cover the pan for a minute or two. Drain off any remaining liquid.

—For even browning: Press the quesadilla with a spatula until it sizzles.

eggs & cheese

Easy Comforts

Eggs Anytime

- Migas (Mexican-Style Eggs)
- Zucchini-Onion Strata
- Goat Cheese and Tomato Omelet
- Asparagus with Poached Eggs
- French Toast
- Cheese Grits and Ham

Cheese Plates

Eggs are a food I truly adore. I've always eaten them, whether they're in or out of vogue. It could be partly in my head, but when I have eggs for breakfast—maybe once a week—I usually have a more productive morning and don't get an 11 a.m. hunger attack.

It seems a shame to limit the perfect protein to breakfast, though, especially if you're the type of person who grabs a bagel or banana most weekday mornings. Mexican-style eggs or a vegetarian strata may have more appeal as options for dinner or a leisurely weekend brunch. The same goes for French toast with maple syrup and crisply cooked bacon.

In writing up these recipes, I noticed that my instructions tended to be lengthy, even when the dish took little time to make. There's a knack involved in making a poached egg or an omelet, but once mastered, it's a lifelong skill that will reward you with many quick and remarkably tasty meals.

Cheese turns up as an ingredient throughout this book, but it's especially prominent in this chapter because of its affinity for eggs. In this chapter you'll also find suggestions for creating cheese plates that can easily serve as a meal.

Easy comforts

Going beyond eggs and cheese, here are some other morning foods that taste good whenever you're hungry.

Oatmeal with extras

Using old-fashioned oats (not instant) or Irish oatmeal, follow the package directions for making a single serving. After removing the oatmeal from the heat, add one or more of these mix-ins:

- Dried Mission figs, dates, or apricots cut into small pieces

- Raisins or dried cranberries

- Honey, brown sugar, or maple syrup to taste

- Pecans, walnuts, or pine nuts

- A touch of cinnamon or nutmeg

My mom's oatmeal

Oatmeal makes a restorative, if unconventional, dinner for one. Sweeten it in one of the ways suggested above, or try the savory alternative I learned from my mother: Prepare the oatmeal with milk instead of water, and season it with butter, salt, and lots of freshly ground black pepper.

Broiled grapefruit & rye toast

Halve a grapefruit and run a serrated knife around the segments to free them. Smear a little honey on top of each half and heat under a broiler for about 5 minutes. Follow the warm grapefruit with a second course of hot, well-buttered rye toast.

Migas (Mexican-Style Eggs)

In Texas, where I grew up—and, in fact, all over the Southwest—this Mexican-style scramble is a familiar favorite. Migas is a Spanish word meaning "rags," referring to the dish's origins as a way to use stale, torn-up tortillas, replaced in this version by tortilla chips. Embellish the migas, if you like, with a green salad, refried beans, or sliced papaya.

2 eggs

2 tablespoons milk or water

1–2 pinches salt

1 teaspoon butter

2 tablespoons chopped onion

2 tablespoons crumbled queso fresco or grated Monterey Jack cheese

1 tablespoon picante sauce or salsa, plus more for serving

Cooked, crumbled bacon, breakfast sausage, or chorizo (optional)

2–3 corn tortilla chips

1 In a small bowl, whisk together the eggs, milk, and salt.

2 Melt the butter in a small skillet over medium-low heat. Add the egg mixture and onion. Cook, stirring until the eggs form soft curds.

3 Remove the skillet from the heat and stir in the cheese and picante sauce. Add the bacon, sausage, or chorizo (if using). Crumble the chips into the eggs. If you like, spoon on more picante sauce at the table.

Zucchini-Onion Strata

1 teaspoon butter, plus more for pan

1 cup loosely packed bread cubes (can be stale)

2 eggs

1 egg white

1/4 teaspoon salt

1/8 teaspoon freshly ground black pepper

1 small zucchini, thinly sliced (about 1 cup)

2 tablespoons chopped scallion, white and green parts

1/3 cup grated cheddar or fontina cheese

1 Preheat the oven to 350°F. Butter a shallow 2-cup baking dish (such as Pyrex). Scatter the bread over the bottom of the pan.

2 In a small bowl, whisk the eggs and egg white with the salt and pepper.

3 Heat a medium skillet over medium heat. Melt 1 teaspoon butter. Add the zucchini and cook, stirring often, until it begins to brown. Add the scallion and cook a minute or so longer. Cool.

4 Spoon the zucchini mixture over the bread cubes. Pour in the eggs, pressing the bread with the back of a fork until well moistened. Sprinkle the cheese over the top. (At this point, the strata can stand at room temperature for up to 1 hour or be refrigerated, covered, for up to 12 hours.)

5 Bake until cooked through and the cheese is lightly browned, about 15 minutes.

Cook's Note

To reheat the second helping, cook at 300°F in an oven or toaster oven until heated through.

Goat Cheese and Tomato Omelet

This is a recipe that takes way longer to describe than to do. If you've never made an omelet, your first one probably won't be a beauty. Once you've mastered the technique, though, you'll have a skill for life.

2 eggs
Large pinch salt
Freshly ground black pepper
1 teaspoon butter
2 tablespoons crumbled fresh goat cheese (about 3/4 ounce)
2–3 tablespoons diced tomato (or quartered grape tomatoes)
2–3 large basil leaves, torn into small pieces

1 In a small bowl, whisk the eggs, salt, pepper, and half an eggshell of water (about 1 tablespoon).

2 Heat a medium sauté pan or omelet pan (see Note) over medium-high heat. Melt the butter, using a heatproof plastic spatula to spread it over the bottom and sides of the pan. Add the eggs to the sizzling butter and count slowly to 5. Moving a fork around the pan in a side-to-side motion, swiftly mix them. Then smooth the eggs evenly over the bottom, tilting the pan as necessary (the eggs should still be liquid enough to make this possible).

3 After a few more seconds, when the eggs are set but still soft on top, remove the skillet from the heat. Sprinkle the goat cheese, tomato, and basil leaves down the center of the eggs. Fold two opposing sides over the middle by about 1 inch. Fold over one of the remaining sides, and then the other to form a neat cylinder. Turn the omelet onto a plate.

Cook's Notes

—Before you start cooking, read the recipe all the way through and have all your ingredients ready.

—To prevent sticking, you need a pan with sloping sides, preferably one that is well seasoned (nonstick is good, too).

Variation

Mushroom-cheddar filling: Sauté 1/2 cup sliced mushrooms and 2 tablespoons chopped shallot or onion in 1 teaspoon butter or olive oil. Season with salt and pepper. Add to the omelet with 2 tablespoons grated cheddar cheese.

Asparagus with Poached Eggs

This classic Italian all-in-one meal should be eaten with crusty bread to catch the delicious sauce created when the egg yolk mingles with the butter and cheese.

8–12 asparagus stalks (about 6 ounces), ends trimmed

1 teaspoon butter

2 eggs

Salt and freshly ground black pepper, to taste

Parmigiano-Reggiano cheese

1 Preheat the broiler. In a skillet large enough to hold the asparagus, bring 1 quart water to a boil over medium-high heat. Cook the asparagus several minutes until tender (test with a fork). Lift the asparagus with a slotted spoon, drain, and transfer to an ovenproof plate. Dot the asparagus with bits of butter.

2 Crack an egg onto a saucer. When the water returns to a slow simmer, slide the egg into it. In the same way, slide the other egg into the water beside the first one. Adjusting the heat so the water bubbles gently, cook the eggs until the whites turn opaque and begin to firm up, 2 to 3 minutes. With the spoon, lift the eggs one by one and place on top of the asparagus.

3 Season the eggs and asparagus to taste with salt and pepper. Grate Parmigiano-Reggiano cheese on top.

4 Place the plate on the top rack of the oven. Prop the door open and broil for a minute or two until the cheese melts and the food is thoroughly hot (keep an eye on it!).

French Toast

French toast is a good idea anytime, but especially when you have bread that's beginning to go stale.

1 egg
1/4 cup milk
1 dash cinnamon or nutmeg
1/8 teaspoon pure vanilla extract
2 (1-inch-thick) slices challah or country bread
1 tablespoon butter

1 Combine the egg, milk, cinnamon, and vanilla in a wide, shallow dish such as a Pyrex pie plate. Whisk until well blended. Soak the bread slices on both sides in the egg mixture.

2 Melt the butter in a medium skillet over medium heat. When it sizzles, fry the bread, turning once, until well browned on both sides. Top with maple syrup, applesauce (see page 215 for a homemade version), fresh fruit, or preserves.

Cheese Grits and Ham

In the rolling hills of southern Indiana, only a stone's throw from Kentucky, springtime brings the annual ritual of the Derby breakfast. A traditional spread consists of country ham, sweetbreads, cheese grits, and pickled Jerusalem artichokes along with foods of the season, such as fresh morels and new potatoes, according to Judy Schad, the maker of renowned goat cheeses sold under her Capriole, Inc. label. You can do a modified solo version, though, any time of day.

3 tablespoons instant grits

1 teaspoon unsalted butter

Large pinch salt

2–3 tablespoons grated Gruyère cheese or cheddar cheese

Freshly ground black or white pepper

**2 thin slices traditional country ham or prosciutto di Parma
(about 1 ounce)**

1 Combine the grits, butter, and salt with 2/3 cup cold water in a microwave-safe dish. Microwave until fairly thick, about 4 minutes.

2 Stir in the cheese and season to taste with pepper. Cover and let stand for 3 minutes.

3 Spoon the grits onto a plate beside the ham.

Cook's Note

To cook on a stovetop, combine the grits, butter, and salt in a small saucepan. Bring to a boil over high heat. Reduce the heat to low, cover, and simmer until the mixture thickens. Proceed as directed above.

Cheese plates

Cheese plates have been gaining ground in American restaurants, where they're sometimes served in lieu of dessert. On the home front, they're a substantial snack or meal you can assemble rather than cook. The idea is to pair a serving of cheese—typically, two ounces—with two or three compatible things. The combinations here happen to taste good together, but, honestly, my intention is not to send you chasing after these particular products. I offer them simply as suggestions to help you begin to explore possibilities for mixing and matching as you put together your own cheese plates.

- Fresh goat cheese—seasoned with herbs or not—or an aged sheep's milk cheese, drizzled with a little extra-virgin olive oil, slices of crusty bread or walnut bread, niçoise or Kalamata olives, ripe tomato wedges, chilled dry white wine

- Aged blue cheese such as Gorgonzola, Stilton, Roquefort, or Cabrales, water crackers, toasted pecans or walnuts, full-bodied red wine or port

- Aged cheddar or Comté cheese, mango or apricot chutney, sourdough bread, fruity red wine, beer, or ale

- Parmigiano-Reggiano chunks, prosciutto di Parma or Serrano ham, fresh or dried figs, coarse country bread, fruity red wine such as Chianti or Barbera

- Camembert, Brie, or fontina d'Aosta, duck pâté slices, ripe pear or apple slices, whole-grain crackers or toast points, big red wine such as Cabernet or Burgundy

- Havarti cheese with dill or caraway seeds, German salami, grainy mustard, cornichons, lightly salted radishes or celery sticks, dark beer

Cook's notes

- If you possibly can, buy your cheese at a specialty store or supermarket with knowledgeable personnel who will cut it to order. Not only will the freshly cut cheese keep longer once you get it home, but the quality of the cheese is likely to be higher.

- Take time to ask questions and to taste the cheeses that interest you before buying. A good cheese monger can suggest wines and other accompaniments for a particular cheese.

snacks & sweets

Speedy Snacks

Savory Treats

- Nachos Deluxe
- Seasoned Pecans
- Marinated Olives
- Homemade Pita Chips and Hummus
- Corn Muffins

Sweet Treats

- Mexican Hot Chocolate
- Chutney Applesauce
- Granola Deluxe
- Spiced Pickled Grapes
- Currant Cookies

When it comes to treats, sweet or savory, we all have our quirks. One day, I crave the pungency of olives or pickled okra. Another, I long for a luscious smear of Gorgonzola or herbed goat cheese on a cracker. For me, "crunchy" is an entire category filled with desirable alternatives: Japanese rice crackers, chilled celery sticks, seasoned toasted nuts, and popcorn, to name a few.

If I have a perfectly ripe pear, nectarine, or plum in my kitchen, it won't last. A pleasant chocolate interlude might center on a hazelnut chocolate bar or a steaming cup of Mexican hot chocolate. And I admit to a fondness for the "fish eyes and glue" texture of tapioca pudding.

Some snacks and sweets in this chapter are assembled in a few minutes, but others take longer. Eat a carrot while you wait, and look forward to having some freshly baked muffins or currant cookies on hand.

Speedy snacks

On the savory side

- Rice cakes or graham crackers spread with peanut butter

- Cottage cheese with scallions or a Boursin-style cheese, scooped up with endive leaves or whole-grain crackers

- Pickled herring or sardines on pumpernickel bread spread with spicy brown mustard

- Half an avocado (pitted but still in its skin), sprinkled with fresh lime juice and salt, and eaten with a spoon

- Hard-cooked eggs with salt and pepper, and bread and butter on the side

- Radishes and baby carrots, sprinkled with sea salt

- Triscuits topped with thin Gouda slices, broiled or microwaved until the cheese melts

On the sweet side

- Frozen grapes or a peeled, frozen banana

- Cantaloupe wedge filled with vanilla ice cream

- A bowl of whole-grain cereal with currants, pecan pieces, and sliced banana

- Chocolate or coffee ice cream sprinkled with wheat germ

- Nutella on toast, or anything really

- The season's best strawberries, drizzled with aged balsamic vinegar

MAKES 1 SERVING
PREP: 5 MINUTES
COOK: 20 SECONDS

Nachos Deluxe

Stave off hunger pangs with this ultra-quick snack. Or, make nachos the centerpiece of a light meal, preceded by cut-up raw veggies and followed by a ripe mango.

1/4 cup refried pinto or black beans
10 corn tortilla chips, baked or regular
10 thin slivers Monterey Jack cheese
5 jalapeño slices, cut in half (see Note)

1 Spread refried beans on the tortilla chips. Lay a sliver of Jack cheese on top of each one.

2 Arrange the nachos in a single layer on a microwave-safe plate. Microwave 15 to 20 seconds, until the cheese melts and the nachos are hot.

Cook's Notes

—Fresh jalapeños are often sold loose in produce departments, allowing you to buy just one or two. Otherwise, buy a small jar of pickled jalapeños, which will keep indefinitely in the refrigerator.

—Alternatively, you can omit the jalapeño and substitute pepper-Jack for the Monterey Jack cheese.

MAKES 1 CUP
PREP: 5 MINUTES
COOK: 15 MINUTES

Seasoned Pecans

Olive oil brings out the rich flavor of the pecans, while maple syrup adds a hint of sweetness. Though I usually make these seasoned pecans in large batches for holiday gifts, this recipe is sized for one lucky person. You can eat them on their own, with a glass of wine, or on a salad.

1 teaspoon maple syrup

2 teaspoons extra-virgin olive oil

1 cup pecans

Salt (preferably kosher)

1 Preheat the oven to 300°F. Combine the maple syrup and olive oil in a small microwave-safe bowl. Microwave until the liquids blend easily, about 20 seconds, or warm over low heat on top of the stove.

2 Line a rimmed baking sheet with aluminum foil. Spread the pecans in a single layer. Drizzle the olive oil mixture over the pecans and stir with a wooden spoon or spatula until well coated. Sprinkle lightly with salt.

3 Toast the pecans until lightly browned and crisp, about 15 minutes, checking often to make sure they do not burn. Store any you do not eat immediately in a tightly sealed container; they'll keep for at least a week.

Variation

Curried Pecans: In a microwave-safe bowl, combine 1 teaspoon peanut or vegetable oil, 1/4 teaspoon curry powder, 1/4 teaspoon sugar, and 1/4 teaspoon salt. Microwave as in step 1. Proceed with steps 2 and 3.

Marinated Olives

You won't believe how much better these taste than plain olives. Refrigerated, they'll keep for several weeks.

1/2 cup unpitted or pitted black or green olives (such as Kalamata, niçoise, or Sicilian)

1 tablespoon extra-virgin olive oil

1 clove garlic, lightly crushed

1/4 teaspoon dried thyme or herbes de Provence

1 broad strip lemon zest (yellow part of the peel) (optional)

1 Rinse the olives under cold running water. Drain well.

2 Place the olives in a small ceramic or glass bowl. Add the olive oil, garlic, thyme, and lemon zest (if using). Let stand at room temperature for at least 2 hours to blend the flavors, or refrigerate. Bring to room temperature before eating.

<u>Cook's Note</u>

To pit olives for a salad or some other use, press each one lightly with the side of a knife blade. Break open the olive with your fingers and pull out the pit.

Homemade Pita Chips and Hummus

Of course you can buy hummus (pita chips are a little more elusive), but it's good to have the option of making a fresh batch, seasoned to your own taste.

2 medium pitas

4 teaspoons olive oil

1/2 teaspoon salt, plus more to taste

1 + 1/2 cups canned chickpeas, drained and rinsed

2 teaspoons tahini (sesame seed paste)

2–3 tablespoons fresh lemon juice

1 small garlic clove

1 Preheat the oven to 425°F. Stack the pitas and cut them into 6 wedges. Place the wedges on a rimmed sheet pan. Brush on both sides with olive oil. Sprinkle lightly with salt. Bake until crisp, about 10 minutes.

2 Meanwhile, combine the chickpeas, tahini, lemon juice, garlic, and 1/2 teaspoon salt in a food processor. Process until fairly smooth, scraping down the sides of the bowl once or twice. If the hummus seems too thick, add 1 or 2 tablespoons water and pulse until incorporated.

3 Place several pita chips on a plate and spoon some of the hummus on top.

Cook's Note

Once cooled, the chips will keep for a couple of days in a recloseable plastic bag. Refrigerated in a covered container, the hummus will keep for about a week; you could also freeze some of it.

SNACKS & SWEETS

211

Corn Muffins

On their own, corn muffins make a great breakfast or anytime snack. They are also nice to eat with beans or a stew.

Butter, for the muffin tin

1 + 1/4 cups unbleached all-purpose flour (see Note)

1/2 cup coarse yellow cornmeal (see Note)

2 tablespoons sugar

2 teaspoons baking powder

1/2 teaspoon salt

2 eggs

1/2 cup milk

3 tablespoons butter, melted

1 Preheat the oven to 425°F. Butter a 12-cup muffin tin. Combine the flour, cornmeal, sugar, baking powder, and salt in a bowl large enough to hold all the ingredients; mix gently with a whisk.

2 In a small bowl, whisk the eggs. Stir in the milk and melted butter.

3 Add the liquid mixture to the dry ingredients and, with a few strokes of a spatula, mix until moistened (do not overmix or the muffins will be tough; it's okay for the mixture to look a bit lumpy).

4 Bake until the muffins rise and are lightly browned on top, about 20 minutes. Cool muffins for a few minutes in the tin before running a knife around each one to loosen and transfer it to a rack.

Cook's Notes

—To measure: Spoon the flour and cornmeal into a measuring cup; do not pack.

—To freeze: Slip muffins into recloseable 1-quart freezer bags (each one will hold two or three). Thaw frozen muffins at room temperature or in the microwave.

Variation

Blueberry Corn Muffins: Wash 1/2 cup blueberries and gently blot dry with a paper towel. Increase sugar to 1/3 cup. Proceed as directed above. Just before baking, fold the blueberries into the muffin batter.

MAKES 1 SERVING
PREP: 2 MINUTES
COOK: 10 MINUTES

Mexican Hot Chocolate

Occasionally I need a hit of chocolate, and making hot chocolate is often the easiest way. Mexican chocolate has a richer flavor than the usual hot cocoa, so I always keep some in the cupboard.

1 ounce Mexican chocolate (see Note)

1/4 cup half-and-half

3/4 cup milk

Ground cinnamon

1 Combine the chocolate and the half-and-half in a small saucepan. Melt the chocolate over low heat, whisking the mixture from time to time.

2 Add the milk. Increase heat to medium-high heat; bring mixture to a boil, whisking often. Sprinkle with cinnamon and pour into a mug.

Cook's Notes

—Mexican chocolate is available in chunks (El Popular) or bars (Goya) in Latino markets and other specialty stores.

—For a frothy treat, after you've added the milk, transfer the chocolate to a blender. Leaving the lid off, blend until the chocolate is frothy.

Chutney Applesauce

4 medium apples, such as Granny Smith or Golden Delicious, peeled, cored, and cut into chunks

1 tablespoon honey

Pinch salt

2 tablespoons mango chutney

1 Combine the apples, honey, and salt in a medium saucepan. Cover the apples to the halfway point with water. Over high heat, bring to a boil. Reduce the heat to low and simmer, covered, until the apples soften, break up, and become applesauce (you can help the process along by crushing the apples with a wooden spoon).

2 Stir in the mango chutney. Eat some of the applesauce while still warm and chill the rest in the refrigerator.

<u>Variation</u>

If you like, replace some of the apples with pears.

Granola Deluxe

My dad is a connoisseur of cereal. First he lays a sturdy base of bran cereal or shredded wheat, then a layer of banana slices and, as the pièce de résistance, a sprinkling of granola. Granola also makes a great topping for ice cream, yogurt, or fruit salad.

4 cups old-fashioned oatmeal (not instant)

1/2 cup toasted wheat germ

1/2 cup shredded sweetened coconut

1 teaspoon cinnamon

1/2 cup chopped pecans or walnuts

1/3 cup honey

1/4 cup vegetable oil

1/2 teaspoon pure vanilla extract

1 cup dried cranberries, raisins, or currants

1 Preheat the oven to 250°F. Dump the oatmeal, wheat germ, coconut, cinnamon, and nuts onto a rimmed sheet pan. Stir to combine.

2 Combine the honey and oil in a small microwave-safe cup. Microwave on high until the honey liquefies and the mixture blends easily, about 20 seconds. Stir in the vanilla.

3 Pour the oil mixture over the dry ingredients. Using a wooden spoon, stir until lightly coated.

4 Bake until the granola is light brown, about 1 hour. Cool in oven, with door ajar, or on a rack. Stir in the dried fruit.

Cook's Note

Stored in an airtight container, the granola will stay fresh for a couple of weeks. Alternatively, you can freeze some in recloseable plastic bags.

MAKES 4 CUPS
PREP: 15 MINUTES
COOK: 10 MINUTES

Spiced Pickled Grapes

Antonia Allegra keeps these cinnamon-spiced grapes on hand to eat with seasoned nuts, with a sandwich, or all alone. "If you're going to someone's house for dinner, tie a ribbon around one of the jars. It makes a great little gift," she adds.

4 cups red seedless grapes, stemmed and washed

1 + 1/2 cups sugar

1 cup white wine vinegar or rice vinegar

4 sticks cinnamon (3 inches each)

2 tablespoons minced onion

1 Place the grapes in 4 half-pint canning jars or in a quart jar. In a small saucepan, combine the sugar, vinegar, cinnamon sticks, and onion. Over high heat, bring the mixture to a boil. Reduce the heat to low, and simmer for 5 minutes.

2 Cool for 5 minutes. Put a cinnamon stick in each jar (or all 4 in one big jar), and pour the liquid over the grapes. Seal the jars, and refrigerate for at least 8 hours before eating.

Cook's Note

The pickled grapes will keep, refrigerated, for up to 1 month.

MAKES ABOUT 6 DOZEN COOKIES
PREP: 30 MINUTES
COOK: 10 MINUTES (PER BATCH)

Currant Cookies

Why should a solo cook miss out on the pleasure of good homemade cookies? You can share some with friends, or freeze some to replenish your cookie jar. These small, buttery cookies are adapted from a recipe by Richard Glavin, a chef who has taught in the culinary arts program at the New School in New York City for many years.

1 cup (2 sticks) butter, softened, plus more for pan

1 + 1/4 cups sugar

1 egg

1 teaspoon pure vanilla extract

2 cups all-purpose flour (see Note)

1/4 teaspoon salt

1 cup currants

1 Preheat the oven to 350°F. Prepare a rimmed sheet pan by coating it with butter, spraying with a nonstick oil spray, or lining it with parchment paper.

2 In the bowl of an electric mixer fitted with the paddle attachment, combine the butter and sugar. Beat on low to medium speed until the mixture is pale yellow and fluffy, turning off the machine and scraping the sides of the bowl at least once. Add the egg and the vanilla and continue to beat until well blended.

3 Combine the flour, salt, and currants in a medium bowl. Add to the other ingredients and mix on low only until incorporated. Transfer the mixture to a 1-gallon recloseable plastic bag or to a smaller bowl (cover with plastic wrap). Chill the dough thoroughly, at least 2 hours in the refrigerator or 30 minutes in the freezer.

4 Pull off small bits of the chilled batter and, between your hands, roll into balls the size of hazelnuts. Place the balls 1 + 1/2 inches apart on the prepared baking sheet. Flatten each one with your thumb (the dough edges will be slightly higher than the depressed middle). Bake until the cookies turn brown around the edges, about 10 minutes. Transfer the cookies to a rack to cool.

Cook's Notes

—Measure the flour by spooning lightly into a measuring cup; do not pack.

—In a well-sealed container, these cookies will keep for at least ten days. You might store some in the freezer and transfer to your cookie jar as needed. Or, you can divide the dough into smaller batches to freeze and bake whenever you like.

index

INDEX